Fifty Favourite
ROSES

Fifty Favourite
ROSES

A choice selection for every gardener

MICHAEL GIBSON

CASSELL

To Dorothy
whose idea this was

Cassell Publishers Limited
Wellington House, 125 Strand
London WC2R 0BB

Text and photographs copyright © Michael Gibson 1995
Designed by Isabel Gillan

First published 1995

British Library Cataloguing in Publication Data
A Catalogue record for this book is available from the British Library

ISBN 0-304-34564-4

Distributed in the United States by
Sterling Publishing Co., Inc.,
387 Park Avenue South, New York, NY 10016-8810

Distributed in Australia by
Capricorn Link (Australia) Pty Ltd
2/13 Carrington Road, Castle Hill, NSW 2154

Typeset by ACC Computing, Somerset, England

Printed and bound in Printing House DELO — Tiskarna
by arrangement with Korotan Ljubljana

HALF TITLE PAGE
'Charles de Mills'

OPPOSITE TITLE PAGE
'Paul Shirville'

TITLE PAGE
'Korresia'

CONTENTS

INTRODUCTION

Since man first learned to write down his thoughts he has, in prose and poetry, praised the rose. The Persians and probably the Chinese, the Greeks with Theophrastus and Sappho, who was the first to describe the rose as the Queen of Flowers, and the Romans with Pliny the Elder and Martial, released a river of admiration which since those days has never ceased to flow. As a result there are examples that can be taken from any period you care to name, Chaucer being picked as representative of the fifteenth century with these lines:

Next the foule nettle, rough and thikke,
The rose waxeth swote, and smothe and soft.

And surely that says it for all time! It removes the need to quote from writings in a similar vein from other authors, even from Shakespeare, who used the rose's beauty symbolically in a thousand ways and showed such surprising knowledge of it both as a plant and as a flower.

Not, however, that everybody did love them, for it is said that Anne of Austria, wife of Louis XIII of France, although otherwise fond of perfumes, reacted so adversely to that of roses that she could not even bear the sight of one in a painting, while Samuel Parsons, American rose grower of the last century, wrote, I do not know on what authority, that: 'No one should venture to sleep with them in his chamber. Some authors of credibility mention instances of death caused by large quantities of roses being left during the night in a sleeping apartment. Thus it is, that the most beautiful things in life contain elements of death'.

However, such strong reactions imply an antipathy toward roses in general rather than a love for or dislike of a particular variety, which can be due to causes much more difficult to describe. Few people like all varieties equally well; some, for instance, seeming to consider it almost indecent if a rose should show its stamens. Others regard the high-centred bloom of the hybrid tea as an abomination and dote on the many-petalled, quartered blooms of the old roses. I have, perhaps, a more catholic taste than some, for I can find beauty in both types, but that does not mean that my critical faculties have deserted me completely, for I still like some roses better than others.

These thoughts went through my head when trying to make up my mind as to which fifty roses I should include in this book, for I know quite well that no other rose-grower is going to agree one hundred per cent with my choice. An eyebrow or two will doubtless be raised at some of the varieties included, understandable as I was not always certain of them myself. Not that any of them were really below the standard I had set, but, just the same, when I decided to include rose 'A', a small voice would immediately be asking why I did not choose rose 'B' instead. There was, to be honest, more than one change of heart as the book progressed.

Before I had even started on it, however, a distinguished rosarian friend of mine, on being told what I was about to undertake, said, 'I don't see how you can do it. Possibly if you confine yourself to fifty of the modern or fifty of the old roses, yes, but not otherwise'.

'Graham Thomas' is probably the best of David Austin's new race of English roses.

What he meant, of course, was that there are too many lovely varieties of rose, something over 20,000 in commerce world-wide, though not all of them can be said to be equally desirable. It hardly needs to be said that I have not grown all of them, but I have, over the years, covered a pretty wide range. From these, with my critical antennae alive and catching every nuance of colour, form, scent and any other quality you can think of, I found that it was just about possible to achieve the impossible. True that in the end there was a short-list of at least another fifty roses that had fought hard to displace some of those I had chosen and, in some cases, had nearly succeeded, but you will not go far wrong with the result as it finally came out. In fact, you will do very well.

All the roses, with the exception of the odd species, gallica and alba, are from the nineteenth and twentieth centuries. All fifty (and most of the other roses that get a passing mention in the text) can be obtained from rose nurseries today, though in a number of cases it may mean going to specialists like David Austin and Peter Beales, or to some of the bigger general rose nurseries that have good old rose lists. And, although it goes against the grain, I must add that certain of the roses, particularly if you have a very small garden, may not be entirely suitable. Each garden is different from the rest and is likely to have differing requirements. Size is not the only consideration, but can be a problem with the bigger roses. Although I have tried to give an idea of the ultimate size of most of the bushes, it is extremely difficult to visualize what this means in reality. An open, airy grower will not look as massive or even overwhelming as a dense, bushy one of exactly the same dimensions so, before you buy, visit gardens to see them all, large and small, in their maturity. You will find that roses speak for themselves and will be their own recommendation, but I hope that this book will be a useful guide and fill in something of the background to many of the best, setting them in the context of their time.

M G

Alba Semi-Plena

So ancient is it, that R × *alba* 'Semi-plena', despite its very unromantic name, could well be Aphrodite's white rose which became the first red rose in the world when stained by her blood as she ran barefoot over the jagged, rocky ground of the Thracian plains to cradle in her arms the mortally wounded Adonis. Or it could be the white rose revered by the pagans which, by man's adaptability and ability to compromise, became in due course the Christian symbol of purity.

This is speculation, of course, but there is no doubt at all that the alba family, to which this rose belongs, is one of the very oldest, with this rose and

The ancient double white alba known as The Jacobite or Bonnie Prince Charlie's Rose.

its double form, 'Maxima', being among its earliest members. It is said that *alba* 'Semi-plena' came to the United Kingdom with the invading Roman armies, and from there, a good deal later, reached the United States. In England they apparently naturalized themselves, at least in the north, though there is scant evidence left that this was so. Some hold that Albion, the Roman name for England, was derived from the white roses the invaders found growing there, but this seems unlikely to be the case if it was the Romans who introduced them. If England was named for a white rose, however, a more probable candidate would be R. *arvensis*, the Field Rose, which is a native species and, if writers from the past are to be relied on, more common than it is today. It seems to me much more likely that the Romans took the name from the White Cliffs of Dover, which would have been their first sight as they approached the English coastline. We will never know the answer, for rose history abounds in such unsubstantiated stories and legends, which is what gives it its fascination.

Where precisely the albas came from in the first place is just as obscure as practically everything else about them. It would seem likely that it was somewhere in the region of the Balkans, although this has never been confirmed. Researches by the botanist C.C. Hurst led him to rather firmer conclusions about their family tree when he deduced that the original alba came from a cross between R. *corymbifera* (a form of the Dog Rose, R. *canina*), and a

Opposite: *'Semi-plena' is the alba rose thought to be the original of the White Rose of York.*

The earliest albas were all white, but 'Céleste' is one in the most delicate pink.

until the autumn, when a fine crop of russet-red hips will be added. There are not too many of the old roses about which this kind of thing could be said, for it must, perhaps rather reluctantly, be admitted that a large proportion of them look extremely tatty by the end of the summer, with badly discoloured leaves and rampant mildew if not black spot. The albas get very high marks in this respect, which helps to make 'Semi-plena' admirable for specimen planting on its own, and it will go well in a mixed planting of other shrubs. It will also make a very good hedge, though it may need one or two of the main shoots cutting back quite hard every so often to keep it bushy low down.

Having kept the Mr Gradgrinds among us happy for a while by covering the facts, let us return briefly to what may well be legend although, as we are rather nearer to the present day than Roman times, it may equally well be fact this time. If you look at the Tudor Rose symbol, you will see that it is actually made up from two roses, a white one contained within a red, and it celebrates the end of the Wars of the Roses and the union of the houses of York and Lancaster. The White Rose of York seems likely to have been 'Semi-plena', while the red rose, the Red Rose of Lancaster, is probably R. *gallica* 'Officinalis'. 'Semi-plena's double form, 'Maxima', mentioned earlier, is also known as the Great Double White and the Jacobite or Bonnie Prince Charlie's Rose. He is reputed to have worn one in his bonnet (supporting the idea that it was naturalized in the north) and his followers are said to have grown it to indicate where their allegiance lay without actually committing themselves by saying so.

As a tailpiece one can add that John Gerard in his *Herbal*, published in 1597, mentions a white rose which, from his description, is almost certainly 'Semi-plena'. More definitely, 'Semi-plena' in the guise of R. × *alba suaveolens*, is one of the varieties planted, in company with damasks, for the production of attar in the Valley of Roses in Bulgaria, though it must be said that its scent, in the United Kingdom at least, is not as strong as one would have expected of a rose used for this purpose. The word 'suaveolens', derived from the French *suave*, meaning 'sweet, pleasant' certainly implies that it would have a significant scent.

damask rose which provided the pollen. To him, the botanical characteristics gave the link, though to the untrained eye there is no obvious similarity, either between the alba and the species or between the alba and a damask rose.

Despite their name, there are more pale pink albas than there are white, although the really old ones, such as the two so far mentioned, are creamy-white. All the family has distinctive foliage, an attractive grey-green colour and, while it is notably free from mildew and black spot, it is not always proof against rose rust. 'Semi-plena' makes a very robust and reasonably upright shrub going up to 6–7ft (1.8–2.1m) and spreading out to maybe 4ft (1.2m). The flowers, which are semi-double, are carried in great profusion in medium-sized clusters and have a delicate fragrance. There is no repeat after the first flush in the second half of June, but the leaves make this an attractive shrub right through

ALBERTINE

The variety 'Albertine' was introduced in 1921 by the firm of Barbier et Cie of Orléans in France, one of the extensive range of ramblers in which they specialized and which included such other long-time favourites as 'Albéric Barbier', 'François Juranville' and 'Léontine Gervais'. No explanation has been forthcoming as to why these Barbier R. *wichuraiana* hybrids flower quite early in the summer whereas the wild rose parent and most of the later hybrids, such as 'Dorothy Perkins' or 'Minnehaha', do not come into bloom until nearly a month later. The fact that these came from an American breeder instead of from France can surely have nothing to do with it.

The Barbier varieties, including 'Albertine', have other differences as well. In some, the growth is much more like that of a climber, stiffer and less pliable than that of a typical rambler. This is particularly true of 'Albertine' which is enormously vigorous – too much so for people who do not realize what it will do and have picked an inappropriate site for it – and will branch out in a most un-rambler-like manner from quite high up along its main shoots in addition to sending up new growth from the base. The coppery-pink flowers are large, too, for the class, wonderfully scented and opening out loosely from pointed buds. They will cover the plant in incredible profusion, which is, of course, why this rose has maintained its popularity for so long despite the fact that there is no second flush in autumn. It can also become a prey to mildew in late summer after the flowering is over, and it cannot be said that the blooms are entirely happy in wet weather. The good points, however, well outnumber the bad, notably the attractive reddish bronze of the early leaves and the fact that they mature to a glossy green that sets off the flowers admirably. The shoots when young are red.

R. *wichuraiana* was one parent of 'Albertine', and the other was 'Mrs Arthur Waddell', a hybrid tea raised in 1909 by Pernet-Ducher in France, its flowers of a reddish-salmon with a rosy-scarlet

'Albertine' is a very vigorous rambler, sweetly scented and flowering in early June.

reverse. The scent of 'Albertine' must have come from the species, for that of 'Mrs Arthur Waddell' was only slight. On a still summer evening 'Albertine' in full flower can be a heady experience for the senses, as its fragrance fills the air.

'Albertine' is so tough and vigorous that it will grow almost anywhere. It is best, however, to keep it away from walls because the comparatively still air there will encourage mildew. Quite frequently one sees this rose offered in nursery lists as a weeping standard, but really it is far from suitable for this. Its shoots are too stiff and strong to hang down or 'weep' naturally and make it difficult to control, even with a special wire frame fixed to the top of the standard stake. Much better to stick to something like 'Dorothy Perkins' or 'Crimson Shower', which were designed by nature specifically for the job.

A good deal has been said about the vigour of 'Albertine' and perhaps it would be a good idea to expand a little on what is meant by this term when describing a rose. In a rambler or climber, as a rule, the greater the vigour the taller the growth. Vigour, however, need not necessarily be linked to size. A miniature rose can be called vigorous if it grows strongly within its own terms of reference. A bushy, freely branching rose can be more vigorous than a tall-growing one, for the latter may simply be spindly in habit.

While still on the subject of vigour, it might be asked whether 'Albertine' will be suitable for growing up a tree, which is one of the loveliest ways of growing either climbers or ramblers. I will let Gordon Edwards, in his book *Roses for Enjoyment*, speak for me on that. He says 'A Cox's Orange Pippin in my old garden which has never done at all well was used as a pillar for 'Albertine'. The way it threaded itself through the apple foliage and revealed its blooms was quite delightful. It shook up the Cox, too, because it forthwith gave a wonderful crop and so continued. This is an illustration of one way to grow ramblers – if not how to get a Cox's Orange Pippin to bear fruit – and to me they look much more natural than when on an artificial arch or fence.' Gordon Edwards, however, failed to warn that

OPPOSITE: *Raised in France early in this century,*
'Albertine' has always been a favourite.

'Albertine', like many other ramblers and climbers, can be grown as a free-standing shrub.

'Albertine', with its fierce armoury of thorns, should not be grown up an apple tree which you are likely to have to climb in order to pick the fruit.

'Albertine' will certainly grow to a good height if encouraged to do so, but on the whole it is best and most floriferous when more or less horizontally trained on a fence or trellis, though pruning can be a problem if it has to be kept within a restricted space. This should be tackled after blooming, when each old flowered shoot can be cut away above the point on it from which a new shoot has grown.

As has been said, 'Albertine' has maintained its place in people's affections for over seventy years because of its spectacular if brief period of glory when in flower each year, and because of its sweet scent. There is, however, another factor that must be taken into account when considering the longevity of 'Albertine' and, indeed, of ramblers in general. Few, if any, new ramblers have been bred after the first twenty years of this century and the lists of varieties in nursery catalogues have scarcely changed. 'Albertine', 'Emily Gray', 'Excelsa', 'Dorothy Perkins', 'Albéric Barbier', 'American Pillar', 'Breeze Hill' and 'Hiawatha' have soldiered on and continue to be bought by those who realize that, in their brief flowering period, ramblers still make an enormous contribution to any garden.

ALOHA

About thirty years ago we were moving to a new house. My knowledge of roses in those days was skimpy and I picked, quite at random from the catalogue of Scott's Merriot nursery, a selection of climbing roses for the walls. Starting at the back of the house and moving round to the front anticlockwise, the list was as follows: 'Paul's Lemon Pillar', 'Golden Showers', 'Climbing Cécile Brunner', 'Meg', 'Aloha', 'Elegance' and – the one real mistake as it ages to a hideous colour – 'Danse du Feu'. Beginner's luck or not, the choice turned out to be a pretty good one, for three out of the seven are among the roses I have chosen for this book. As they are being covered in alphabetical order, the first of the three climbers to be described must be 'Aloha'.

The blooms of 'Aloha' are of old rose form.

In view of the fact that it is a very large country with a wide range of climatic conditions, some of which must approximate to that of the United Kingdom, it may seem puzzling at first that few new rose varieties from America cross the Atlantic and thrive. However, when one learns that many of them are raised in the sunshine of California, the reasons become clearer. In the same way many excellent roses raised on the Riviera, at the Meilland Nursery for instance, (always excepting 'Peace') do not take kindly to the comparatively cold and rainy climate of the United Kingdom. For a rose from America or France (or from any of the other Mediterranean countries) to gain one of the top awards in northern European trials is a rare occurrence, while those from the United Kingdom, from Germany and from Holland feature quite frequently in the lists. 'Aloha', although it won no awards, is one of the few American roses to have made the transition successfully, even if it has taken some time for its great qualities to be recognized. It dates from 1949, but it is only in recent years that its true worth is being appreciated. Having praised it many, many times in books and magazines since the time I first discovered it, I like to think that I have played at least a small part in bringing it to the fore.

It is a versatile rose as it can be used as a fairly upright shrub growing to about 4ft (1.2m) in height (making it suitable for a hedge or for planting in a mixed border), or as a vigorous but not especially tall

OPPOSITE: *As a slow-growing climber, 'Aloha' will reach about 12ft (3.6m); as a shrub, 4ft (1.2m).*

One parent of 'Aloha' was 'New Dawn'; the other,
'Mercedes Gallart', is seen here.

climber. It is often recommended as a pillar rose and can be very effective when used in this way, especially as it will flower quite well at all levels. Any pillar rose will flower better if the shoots are trained in a spiral round the support, which will encourage the production of flowering side shoots, but with 'Aloha' this kind of training must be started very early. The shoots are strong and not especially pliable after their first year, so that pointing them in the right direction must begin when they are young.

The magnificent flowers of 'Aloha' have inherited many of their qualities from one parent, 'Mercedes Gallart', the flowers of which are described in *Modern Roses* as being 'Very large, double, very fragrant, deep pink, base yellow; long, strong stems.' This could almost be a description of 'Aloha' itself, but the fact that they are almost rain-proof should be added. To achieve 'Aloha', the American breeder, Eugene Boerner, crossed 'Mercedes Gallart' with 'New Dawn', an inspired combination.

The flowers of 'Aloha' come, surprisingly, from rather unattractive and unpromising-looking buds.

These seem to have been chopped off at the tips, rather like those found on some of the old roses, denoting shortish centre petals. The fully expanded blooms of 'Aloha' do, as a matter of fact, more closely resemble one of the old roses or a paeony than those of a hybrid tea – they are literally bursting with petals.

As a climber on a wall, which is the way I first grew it, 'Aloha' can take some time to get moving. With me it took six to seven years to climb up twelve feet of wall, which is actually a better performance than I have seen elsewhere. It is smothered with its fine big blooms in June and, with a number coming in between, there is a good display in early autumn as well. The one drawback it has as a climber is that individual flowers and trusses of bloom come on long, strong and almost thornless stems. After rain the blooms become laden with water, which they cope with very well, but it does cause them to hang out a considerable distance from the wall. It looks a bit untidy, but on the other hand the good stems mean that 'Aloha' makes an excellent cut flower, and it will last a long time in water.

Until perhaps three years ago (by which time I had been growing it for almost thirty years) I would have said that 'Aloha' was a variety that was completely disease-free, its bright green, glossy foliage always immaculate. It is still quite free from mildew and black spot, but all of a sudden rust has appeared. This has coincided with the spread of rust westward across the United Kingdom in recent years and 'Aloha' is not the only rose in my garden to be showing signs of it for the first time. Spraying with a rust fungicide does keep the spores at bay to a large extent, but it has been disappointing, to say the least, to find this Achilles' heel on what I had always considered one of the nearly perfect roses. I ought to add that cuttings I have taken from the climber to grow as shrubs have so far remained healthy. Perhaps the climber is just getting tired.

BALLERINA

This rose makes a dense, rounded shrub, usually growing to about 3–4ft (1–1.2m) tall and about as much across, though I have seen it about a foot or so larger all round in situations where it is obviously exceptionally happy. The many flowering shoots carry large heads of small, single flowers, light pink and with a white eye, resembling and often compared with apple blossom. The glossy leaves are bright green and generally healthy, though black spot is by no means unknown. There is also a good show of bloom in the autumn, when extra vigorous basal shoots may be sent up, all of which make it a rose for a low hedge or for planting in clumps. It is, in addition, often included nowadays among the fashionable ground cover varieties, although it came into existence long before the term ground cover rose was thought of – except perhaps for the varieties 'Max Graf' and R. × *paulii*.

Nobody knows what the parentage of 'Ballerina' may be. It came from the Pemberton nursery after Joseph Pemberton's death and was probably one of his seedlings. He was, of course, the raiser of the hybrid musk group of roses, and when he died his sister Florence carried on the nursery for a while until it was taken over by their foreman, J.A. Bentall, prior to setting up on his own. It was Bentall who actually introduced 'Ballerina' in 1937, the same year that the German nurseryman, Peter Lambert (who had earlier bred the shrub rose 'Trier' which was the foundation variety of the hybrid musk line), introduced a rose very similar to 'Ballerina' called 'Mozart'. The flowers of this were of a rather deeper pink than those of 'Ballerina', but otherwise they are

'Ballerina', an attractive, low-growing shrub, will cover quite a lot of ground.

so alike that it seems possible that they were sister seedlings. The rose Bentall introduced may have come originally from Lambert, with whom Pemberton already had a working relationship.

'Ballerina' itself is often classed as a hybrid musk for no reason that I can see other than that it came from the Pemberton stable. He bred a good many other kinds of rose apart from those that made him famous, and the hybrid musks themselves were a pretty mixed bag, being sold at first as hybrid teas. When entered as such in a show of the National Rose Society (not yet Royal) the then secretary would have none of this and the story goes that it was he who suggested the name hybrid musk simply because of the new roses' good scent. It was intended as a stop-gap until something better was thought of, for they had only the remotest connection with the true musk rose, but the name stuck. All of which indicates that there was a somewhat happy-go-lucky approach to classification and to family trees in the Pemberton breeding establishment, although the parents of most of the hybrid musks are known. 'Ballerina' is a sad orphan in this happy family.

When Bentall finally put 'Ballerina' on the market it hardly caused a ripple. In fact very little notice was taken of it for something like sixty years until, early in the 1960s, Fryer's Nurseries put it in their catalogue and really began to promote it. A firm largely existing at that time on a diet of high-quality hybrid teas and floribundas, Fryer's seemed to have, and indeed still has, a habit of producing unexpected rabbits out of their hat for, apart from 'Ballerina', they have over the years come up with 'Fred Loads', 'Sally Holmes', 'Nozomi' and, most recently, with 'Flower Carpet'.

In their 1964 catalogue they devoted a whole page to 'Ballerina'. 'Imagine', the text of this read, 'huge trusses of flowers in hydrangea-like heads all summer long. The glorious pink blooms are a joy to behold, so light and dainty they give no idea of the weight of bloom which clothes these attractive bushes. Trouble-free with a variety of uses. We are proud to offer this fine variety to our customers at

7/6 each, 84/- dozen
Standards 15/- each'

OPPOSITE: *This picture shows why the blooms of 'Ballerina' are often compared to apple blossom.*

No one today would quarrel with the above, particularly the price, and the advertisement gives the first suggestion for a use of 'Ballerina' which is enormously popular today. It makes an absolutely first-rate standard rose, forming an excellent head, much better than that of many hybrid teas or floribunda roses.

Surprisingly for such a good and popular rose, 'Ballerina' does not appear to have been used very much in the breeding of other varieties. The only offspring of which I am aware closely resembles it, except that the light pink of the flowers has been replaced by a deep carmine, though still with the white eye. This rose is 'Marjorie Fair', bred by Jack Harkness in 1977 from 'Ballerina' × 'Baby Faurax'. It can be used in all the same ways as 'Ballerina', although its much stronger colour means that a little more care is needed when planning its juxtaposition in relation to other plants.

'Ballerina' is one of the modern shrub roses that makes a fine standard.

BANKSIAN DOUBLE YELLOW

Should you see from a distance the south wall of a house, a wall perhaps 30ft (9m) tall and as much across, apparently covered by a soft, primrose yellow cloud, this is likely to be your first glimpse of *R. banksiae* 'Lutea', the double yellow Banksian rose. For once it gets away after what may be a slow start, with some reluctance to flower, the slender but immensely vigorous, almost thornless shoots of this rose will spread far and wide, covered in early sum-

There are four different forms of the Chinese Banksian rose. This is the double white.

mer with shiny, rather narrow leaves and clusters of the most enchanting, small, cupped, double yellow flowers. If they were more strongly scented they would be near to perfection, but for sheer profligacy with its flowers the Banksian Double Yellow would be hard to beat.

Although this rose is usually given a Latin name, there can be little doubt that it is of garden origin, first reported to have been seen in Calcutta Botanic Garden, to which it had been brought from China. It came to the attention of the Royal Horticultural Society, who asked J.D. Parks to put it on his shopping list for his next flower-hunting trip to the Far East. He brought it back and it bloomed for the first time in England in 1824.

Perhaps because of the slenderness of the light green stems, the Banksian Double Yellow is difficult to propagate by budding, so that plants are usually grafted. It blooms on side shoots of the previous year's growth, so as little pruning as possible should be done or the flowering shoots may be cut away. Use the secateurs only to keep it within bounds or if frost has damaged some of the shoots. Frost can be a problem unless a sheltered site is chosen, though it should be noted the Double Yellow is the hardiest of four Banksian varieties.

There is, in fact, another yellow one, *R. banksiae* 'Lutescens', which has single flowers with the scent of violets, but it did not appear in England until 1870, introduced by Sir Thomas Hanbury, who grew it in his Riviera garden, La Mortola. However, it is not really hardy in the UK climate. The same applies to the other two Banksians, the first of which

The most popular Banksian climber is the double yellow, which needs a warm wall.

is the double white, *R. banksiae* 'Banksiae'. This was at first thought to be the original wild form, brought to the West from Canton in 1807 by William Kerr. It was discovered, however, that it sets no seed and so is incapable of propagating itself, meaning that the others can hardly be descended from it. Nevertheless, it has another claim to fame, for this is the rose that is said to have rooted from a cutting in the yard of the Rose Inn in Tombstone, Arizona, growing in time to be the 'Largest Rose in the World'. It has a girth of 4ft 10in (1.5m) at the base and the whole thing covers an area of 4620sq ft (429sq m) supported by fifty-four posts and the walls of the inn. In spring it is said to resemble a 'giant snowbank glistening in the sun'. In that climate it blooms in April instead of May, the month in which its yellow cousin blooms in the United Kingdom.

While the Double Yellow is unlikely to reach the proportions just described, it still managed, for instance, to reach something between 30–40ft (9–12m) in height on one of the walls of the burned-out ruins of Nymans in Sussex, and can be seen in similar good form on the walls of other old country houses but, as I mentioned earlier, it is a slow starter. If you do plant it yourself, be patient. My own took all of five years before it came into flower, and I would hardly call it a giant, even now.

Finally a brief word about the fourth Banksian rose, *R. banksiae* 'Normalis'. Single, white and fragrant, it is almost certainly the true species, which was first identified and sent to Europe in 1877. There is a story that it had arrived much earlier and was growing on the wall of Megginch Castle, Strathspey, Scotland, brought from China by a member of the Drummond family in 1796. As it never flowered, however, nobody could say what it was until it was at last identified in 1905, over one hundred years after its arrival. It was the single white form of the Banksian rose that gave the group its identity, being named after Lady Banks, wife of Sir Joseph Banks, explorer, plant hunter and President of the Royal Horticultural Society.

BLUSH RAMBLER

This is a rose not seen nearly as much as it should be, for it is one of the loveliest of ramblers, introduced by B.R. Cant in 1903, having been raised from a cross between 'Crimson Rambler' and 'The Garland'. The cupped, soft pink flowers, pleasantly scented, come with tremendous freedom, lasting from June on into July, though, being a rambler, there is no repeat. Some multiflora ramblers can be a little coarse in many respects, particularly in the foliage, but here the light green leaves leave nothing to be desired. Almost thornless, it will grow with vigour to 15 ft (4.5 m) or so, and thus is tall enough for an arch or pergola. I have also seen it used to great effect as a shrub on its own, making use, however, of something to give it some support.

Apart from using this rose as described above, it will make a fine weeping standard, or it can be employed to frame one of those high-rise abodes for spiders and insects, otherwise known as a bower. Grown on a frame of rustic poles or against a fence, the soft colouring of its flowers will make a most pleasing background for any stronger-coloured plants that may be planted in front of it, and it will look extremely well, too, against the dark, shiny foliage if allowed to ramble through some evergreen shrub such as a holly.

It is sometimes confused with 'Kew Rambler', raised at Kew in 1912, and there is some resemblance between the two roses. However, the 'Kew Rambler' flowers are single and the leaves have a greyish tint passed on from *R. soulieana*, its pollen parent. In addition, the flowers are distinctly lighter in the centre.

'Blush Rambler' is too rarely seen for such a fine rose. It will scale a small tree.

'Blush Rambler' was introduced during the peak period for the popularity of the rambler roses, the end of the nineteenth century and the beginning of the twentieth. Much encouraged by the writings of Gertrude Jekyll, a number of good varieties were raised in the United Kingdom, among them 'Gold-finch' from Paul in 1907 and 'Paul's Scarlet' in 1918, together with 'Sander's White' from Sander in 1912 and 'Emily Gray', introduced by B.R. Cant in 1918 and raised by an amateur, Dr A.H. Williams, President of the National Rose Society in 1933–4. He was also responsible for breeding that charming rambler

'Blushing Lucy', but that was not until 1938. 'Emily Gray' is the one that has survived in the lists, probably because of its chamois yellow colouring, unique among ramblers.

However, expanding on what was said on page 13 when discussing 'Albertine', the output in Britain was dwarfed by that of France and the United States. The number of outstanding ramblers from Barbier et Cie of Orléans was quite phenomenal and from among many others one could select as examples 'Albéric Barbier' (1900), 'Paul Transon' (1901), 'Léontine Gervais' (1903), 'François Juranville' (1906), 'Alexander Girault' (1909), 'Auguste Gervais' (1918) and, of course, 'Albertine' (1921). The Barbier output was almost matched by that of M.H. Walsh of Woods Hole, Massachusetts, USA, with 'Debutante' of 1902, 'Hiawatha' (1904), 'Minnehaha' and 'Lady Gay' (1905), 'Evangeline' (1906) and 'Excelsa'

(1909). In addition, 'Jersey Beauty' came from W.A. Manda in 1899, 'Dorothy Perkins' from Jackson & Perkins in 1901 and 'Dr W. Van Fleet' in 1910.

These were the main protagonists of the period, though 'Veilchenblau', raised by J.C. Schmidt in Germany in 1909, should not be left out of any list of ramblers of the period as it is still quite widely grown.

If 'Blush Rambler' had arrived on the scene just one year earlier it would certainly have been extolled in Gertrude Jekyll's *Roses for English Gardens*, for ramblers and their uses were one of her passions and this became one of her favourites. It came instead one year after the book was published and so missed the chance of being brought to the notice of her hundreds of followers, which might in turn have made it better known today. While not claiming to be a second Jekyll, perhaps what I say here may do a little to rectify the matter.

In this picture 'Blush Rambler' has been trained on a wooden frame at Upton Grey, a fully restored Jekyll garden.

CANARY BIRD

This is the second rose in flower in my garden each April, the first being the not dissimilar 'Helen Knight' which, however, is growing against one wall of the house so that the heat of the wall gives it an unfair advantage. Both roses, with their bright yellow, single flowers on the shortest of stems all along great arching shoots, welcome in the rose season in the most enchanting way.

'Canary Bird' will make a large, open shrub growing to about 7 × 7ft (2.1 × 2.1m). Like all species roses, it should not be pruned, which means it should never be cut back to fit a space for which it

The bright yellow, single blooms of 'Canary Bird' are among the first to open each year.

has grown too large. The major charm of these wild roses is the long, curving, blossom-laden shoots and this is destroyed if they are cut back. They should be given their head and only dead or diseased wood be removed as and when it is seen.

If your garden is not really big enough for the shrub, go for 'Canary Bird' in standard form, as stocked by many nurseries, for grown thus it will not be nearly as vigorous. It will, nevertheless, make a large head, more on a par with that of a weeping standard than one formed from a hybrid tea or floribunda; so a stake stronger than those supplied for conventional standards is really needed. However you choose to grow it, if your space is limited remember that this rose flowers only from the end of April (or a little earlier in a good year) until the end of May or early June. After that, although the ferny foliage is attractive, there will be no further flowers. A few hips, deep red or nearly black, may form in the autumn, but they are not showy as are those of many other species, such as R. *moyesii*. One cannot argue with the fact that one of the modern shrub roses that is fully recurrent may be more desirable to give a continuity of colour, but if you choose one instead of 'Canary Bird' you may be missing something that really lifts the heart in spring.

Apart from 'Canary Bird', there are quite a large number of early-flowering species roses with yellow single flowers. They include 'Helen Knight' already mentioned, R. *hugonis*, R. *primula*, R. *ecae*, R. *foetida* and various hybrids of R. *pimpinellifolia*, such as 'Ormiston Roy', 'Frühlingsgold' and R. *pimpinellifolia* 'Altaica'. So why settle on 'Canary Bird'?

*For a garden of modest size, the best way to grow 'Canary Bird'
is as a standard.*

Well, as good a reason as any is that 'Canary Bird' can match if not out-perform any of the others in its display of flowers and it is by far the easiest to buy. Many nurseries, with only a token number of shrub roses in their catalogue, stock 'Canary Bird' and, as mentioned, often in standard form. For most of the other species, with the possible exception of 'Frühlingsgold', you would have to order from a nursery that specializes in old roses, such as Peter Beales or David Austin; but it might be of interest to describe these briefly here, for each one has its points and all are worth considering before settling to take the easy way out and go for 'Canary Bird'.

R. *hugonis* may well be one of the parents of 'Canary Bird' (of this, more later) and was discovered in China around the turn of the century by the Rev. Hugh Scanlon, known as Father Hugh. The modern plants originate from seed he sent back which was germinated at Kew Gardens, and introduced in 1908 by James Veitch and Sons of Chelsea, when it became popular in both the United Kingdom and America. The flowers, a much paler yellow than those of 'Canary Bird', appear in equal profusion, but the petals often fail to unfurl properly, marring the over-all effect. R. *primula*, also from China and known as the 'Incense Rose' because of its aromatic leaves, is also a fairly pale, primrose-yellow and makes a smaller bush than those so far described. It is about the same size, 5 × 4ft (1.5 × 1.2m), as a rose with a name that no one knows how to pronounce, R. *ecae*. (This does, in fact, derive from the initials of the wife of Dr J.E.T. Aitchison, the botanist who

For sheer profusion of bloom, 'Canary Bird' can rival any other rose.

the pimpinellifolia hybrid 'Ormiston Roy', which will grow to no more than 4ft (1.2m) tall, bearing a few of its clear yellow flowers in late summer as well as in the first June flush. It is quite modern, dating from 1938, and is one of the parents of 'Golden Wings' (see page 66). Finally we come to two other pimpinellifolia hybrids, 'Frühlingsgold', at 7 × 5 ft (2.1 × 1.5 m) quite a giant, and with much larger, pale yellow flowers than any of the others so far discussed, and 'Altaica' from the Altai mountains on the border between Russia and Mongolia, which means it is a rose of great hardiness. It has creamy-white, single blooms and great elegance.

If I had wanted to be comprehensive, I could also have mentioned 'Dunwichensis', 'Golden Cherso-nese', 'Cantabridgiensis' and 'Headleyensis', to say nothing of the early yellows with double flowers such as 'Harison's Yellow', but this piece is supposed to be about 'Canary Bird' and I have been deflected long enough.

'Canary Bird', although apparently bearing all the physical attributes of a species rose, is now considered to be a hybrid, possibly raised in a botanic garden, a cross between *R. hugonis* and another rose from China, *R. xanthina*. At one time it was sold as *R. xanthina* 'Spontanea' under the impression that it was the wild type of *R. xanthina*, but the latter is a rose with double flowers which has, nevertheless, been granted the specific name. All very confusing, the more so as 'Canary Bird' only seems to have been around since 1906, so the records of its ancestry can hardly be buried in antiquity. It seems that botanic gardens as well as some nurseries were not always meticulous in keeping records of their breeding programmes. However that may be, if your soil is reasonably light, do try 'Canary Bird'. Grow some of the others too, if you wish, but not instead of it. Even so, a warning should be sounded. 'Canary Bird', like *R. hugonis* before it, is not too happy on cold, heavy soils, when die-back can occur.

discovered it, which were E.C.A.) It is more upright in habit than most of the species we have been discussing and might be the one to choose if lack of space is a prime consideration. The flowers are of a particularly brilliant yellow, as are those of *R. foetida*, which a number of people might wish to grow because of its historical associations as the parent of 'Soleil d'Or', our first yellow garden rose from which all others are descended. However, black spot will be a problem with this rather unpredictable, untidy grower. In contrast, and of compact habit, is

CÉCILE BRUNNER

A quite exquisite little rose, the blooms of which, borne freely on a light, airy bush about 3ft (1m) in height, are of a delicate pink, in bud the size of thimbles, like those of a miniature hybrid tea with its scrolled centre – the Bambi of the rose world. More commonly known as the Sweetheart Rose, it was introduced by Pernet-Ducher of Lyon in 1881. In some catalogues classed as a China rose (presumably because with its long, pointed leaves and open style of growth it does rather resemble that family), it really should be grouped with the polyanthas. It is thought to be a cross between one of that group and the hybrid tea 'Mme de Tartas', but it seems to be reluctant to hand on its outstanding qualities to future generations by hybridizing in its turn with anything else. Jack Harkness found it never set seed, but the Dutch breeder, de Vink, is on record as using it to produce some of his miniatures, including the outstanding 'Cinderella'. Otherwise the records show a blank. Fragrance cannot be counted among 'Cécile Brunner's attributes, but it has just about everything else needed for a rose to fill a small bed or mix with other plants, providing autumn flowers as well as those in spring.

Although I have some experience of growing 'Cécile Brunner' in bush form, I have a far more extensive acquaintance with the plant as a climbing sport, which brings about an almost unbelievable transformation. The flowers remain the same, though perhaps a fraction bigger, but the long, flexible, plum-red shoots that it sends out with unrestricted extravagance from the base can grow 10ft in a season. A 'Climbing Cécile Brunner' covers the entire side wall of my house, going up probably to 20ft (6m) and spreading out sideways by about the same. Each June it is a sight to behold, the shoots and leaves (and the wall) difficult to see beneath the smother of blooms. This will continue for several weeks and there will always be some flowers throughout the remaining summer months before a second, less enthusiastic flush in late August or September. Another 'Climbing Cécile Brunner'

In its bush form 'Cécile Brunner' is a modest grower, but as a climber it is rampant.

The flower buds of 'Cécile Brunner' are thimble sized, but the blooms open loosely.

sends its shoots wandering up through a truly gigantic, free-standing Moroccan Broom (*Cytisus battandieri*) at the bottom of our garden. The latter is 15ft (4.5m) high and 20ft (6m) across (accurately measured, as I began to doubt my own eyes) and the combination of the soft yellow pineapple-like flowers of the broom and the soft pink of the rose is really quite outstanding. And the pineapple scent of the broom more than makes up for the faint fragrance that comes from the rose: totally overwhelms it, in fact, and every other scent in the garden.

With its healthy foliage, which never seems to need spraying, this is an ideal rose for a fairly large arch, catenary or pergola in addition to the two uses to which I have put it, and it seems to revel in rather poor dry soil.

The bush form of 'Cécile Brunner' has produced at least one sport, 'White Cécile Brunner', the white flowers of which are lemon-tinted in the centre. Coral-pink 'Mme Jules Thibaud' is said to be another sport, while 'Perle d'Or', raised by Dubreuil in 1883, is sometimes wrongly referred to as 'Yellow

Cécile Brunner'. One can understand why, for flowers are of a roughly similar size, the pink, however, being replaced by light orange but the bush is much more vigorous as a rule and more upright in growth. There is, too, a pleasing fragrance, possibly from the tea rose parent, 'Mme Falcot'. The other parent was, as with 'Cécile Brunner', a polyantha.

Yet another rose that some contend is a sport of 'Cécile Brunner' is 'Bloomfield Abundance'. The flowers closely resemble each other in colour, shape and size, except that those of 'Bloomfield Abundance' have long, feathery tips to the sepals. The bush, however, lacks the lightness and elegance of 'Cécile Brunner'. It is upright, can easily grow to 6ft (1.8m), and in the autumn sends up the most enormous shoots bearing dozens of blooms – it is indeed a most impressive sight.

Bean, in the rose section of *Trees and Shrubs Hardy in the British Isles*, whose authority few would normally question, says of 'Bloomfield Abundance': 'The plant known in British gardens as 'Bloomfield Abundance' is possibly a sport of 'Cécile Brunner', but until an established bush of 'Cécile Brunner' sports again, or an accepted 'Bloomfield Abundance' reverts, there is no conclusive evidence available; the type 'Bloomfield Abundance' was raised in the USA with a stated parentage of Hybrid Teas.' The parentage referred to and given in *Modern Roses* is 'Sylvia' × 'Dorothy Page Roberts'.

As against this, Jack Harkness can be quoted as saying: 'It has long been obvious to nurserymen who see their stock of 'Cécile Brunner' suddenly change into 'Bloomfield Abundance' that the parentage in *Modern Roses* cannot possibly be right ... whatever the books say, it is a sport of 'Cécile Brunner'.

Peter Beales agrees with Jack Harkness, adding that it would be extremely rare for a sport to be so stable. And as a final twist to the conundrum (if conundrums can have twists) I will give just one more quote, this time from the late Dean M. Ross, writing on 'Cécile Brunner' in the *Bulletin* of the Historic Roses Group of the Royal National Rose Society. 'Let us now turn', he writes, 'to George C. Thomas Jr., who bred the 'Bloomfield' series of roses. In 1930 he published *The Practical Book of Outdoor Rose Growing*. On page 222 ... there is a black and white photograph of the bush ['Bloomfield Abundance'] and, with the aid of a magnifying glass it is obvious that the sepals of the buds do not have the characteristic wings or leaves. Obviously, what everyone grows now is not the original 'Bloomfield Abundance'. What is it? We will probably never know, but it would be a very interesting line of research.'

Truly the rose historian gets to know how Christopher Columbus must have felt when setting out on his most famous voyage: not sure where he was going and, when he got there, not sure where he was.

The early flowering of 'Climbing Cécile Brunner' is spectacular, the autumn repeat more restrained.

CHARLES DE MILLS

Although belonging to the oldest family of garden roses – the gallicas – nobody knows just when 'Charles de Mills' first appeared on the scene. It finds no place in Rivers's *The Rose Amateurs' Guide* (1840) or in Paul's *The Rose Garden* of eight years later, and neither would have ignored such a beautiful and remarkable-looking rose if it had been in existence. The flowers are really something very special but open from buds that look far from promising, appearing to have had the tips sliced off,

'Charles de Mills' has some of the most striking flowers of all the old roses.

making them goblet shaped. But as the petals unfurl, what a transformation! Crammed with crimson petals, they are at first cupped and then open out quite flat but with the petals infolded on themselves, showing better, perhaps, than any other rose just what is meant by a bloom being 'quartered', for the folds divide the flowers into four distinct sections. Some 4in (10cm) across, they come with great freedom for about three to four weeks in early summer. Little scent is discernible, but they stand up to wet weather remarkably well for a rose with blooms containing so many petals. Its striking flowers have led to its alternative name of 'Bizarre Triomphant' in France, a country in which it is likely to have originated, along with many other nineteenth-century gallica roses.

In growth it is fairly typical of the family, twiggy and upright, reaching about 4ft (1.2m) on average. The stems are covered in more bristles than thorns, again a gallica characteristic, as are the rather rough, coarse-looking leaves. When the flowers are out you will hardly notice these, but with all of this family they are a distinct drawback late in the season as they age badly and may succumb to mildew. For this reason gallicas are best mingled with other kinds and 'Charles de Mills' looks splendid with strong pink varieties or in a border of mixed plants. Take care, however, if you do mix it in with other things, that it is grown on a rootstock and not on its own roots. All gallicas sucker freely and 'Charles de Mills' is no exception. In my own garden a plant grafted on to a rootstock was probably planted rather deeper than it should have been and in time put out its own roots.

Not more than about 4ft (1.2m) tall, 'Charles de Mills' is a good rose for a small garden.

Suckers came up some way from the parent plant and, unwisely, I thought it would be nice to have a few more of one of my favourite old roses about the place. That was all of twenty years ago and I am still battling with suckers up to 30ft (9m) from the original planting, which invariably choose to come up in the middle of something else. A weedkiller that works through the roots, tried first in some trepidation as I was not sure how far back along the roots it would travel, seems only to check things temporarily. These suckers are second only in aggression to those of the pimpinellifolia family, which travel with the speed of an underground train, though rather more silently.

'Charles de Mills' illustrates graphically the difference between the formation of the blooms of many of the old roses and those most highly prized today. Without exception, the double roses from earliest days until the middle of the last century or a little later had short centre petals and much longer outer ones. This meant that the blooms would open out cupped or goblet-shaped. With roses such as the centifolias they might stay this way, but others, among them 'Charles de Mills' and many other gallicas, would then open out flat. It was not until the coming of the tea rose from China in the last century that a change gradually came about. The teas had much longer centre petals and the offspring of older roses when crossed with them began to change their form. Careful selection by breeders encouraged this and gradually the hybrid perpetuals and after them the hybrid teas showed the shape of things to come. The high, conical centre, so much admired today, especially on the show bench, is entirely man-made and not a natural phenomenon. Hold a bloom of 'Charles de Mills' next to one of a typical modern show rose, 'Stephanie Diane' for instance, and one would hardly think they were of the same genus.

COMPASSION

This is certainly the most outstanding climber raised in recent years, the brainchild – a phrase used advisedly – of its raiser, Jack Harkness, who used both instinct and intelligence based on long experience in his approach to creating new varieties. It follows the modern trend in that it is not too rampant a grower, so that it will suit gardens of modest size. It is, nevertheless, very vigorous, and has the useful habit of sending up a lot of new growth from the base. For growing on a pillar this can be a disadvantage as there may be too much growth to be accommodated comfortably, but otherwise 'Compassion' is very much to be desired and, with so many shoots, it is always covered with its fine, dark green, glossy, healthy leaves from top to bottom, avoiding the rather leggy lower regions of some otherwise estimable climbers. It also means that it can stand on its own as a shrub if you choose to use it in this way.

However, it is in its climbing form that it really comes into its own, going up probably to about 10ft (3m) and producing with great freedom beautifully shaped, hybrid tea-type flowers of apricot pink with a soft orange glow in the centre – a most attractive combination. The scent, too, is outstanding.

'Compassion' has two rather unlikely parents, 'White Cockade', which is an admirable rose but could only be called a semi-climber, and the less-than-admirable, mildew-prone hybrid tea 'Prima Ballerina', which for some unfathomable reason seems to have been a much more successful parent of other roses than it has been as a garden variety – in my experience at any rate. 'Compassion' has two

The blooms of 'Compassion' are not only beautifully shaped but they are fragrant, too.

main flushes of bloom, the first starting at the beginning of June and the second in September, but there will always be flowers in between. The later flowering will often produce richer colours, a not uncommon phenomenon with roses.

A success overseas as well as in the United Kingdom, 'Compassion' is known in France as 'Belle de Londres'. Introduced in 1973, it had been awarded a Trial Ground Certificate in the RNRS trials in 1972 and the Edland Medal for fragrance in the year of its launching. In addition there was a fragrance award in the Hague, an All Germany Rose selection, and Gold Medals in Baden-Baden and Geneva. It also has the unique distinction of gaining a Gold Medal two years running in the Trials at Orléans, having, through a slip-up, been entered twice. Only the first award was allowed to count, but it did at least show that the judging was consistent.

The name 'Compassion' derives from the United Kingdom welfare organization REHAB, and a proportion of the receipts from the initial sales went to this charity.

In 1980 a sport of 'Compassion' was launched by the Harkness nurseries. This was 'Highfield', another climber but differing from its parent in the colour of its flowers, which are a soft yellow though occasionally the odd one will revert. It is perhaps not quite so vigorous as 'Compassion', but is suitable for a fence, pillar or wall. This one was named for the sixtieth anniversary of the Highfield Nurseries in

Gloucestershire, but the continuing story of 'Compassion' does not end with this one sport. It has been introduced into the Harkness breeding lines and been eminently successful as the parent of two outstanding hybrid teas, 'Paul Shirville' and 'Rosemary Harkness'. More recently has come 'High Hopes', another climber of moderate vigour. In my garden this is in its first year and so it is a little early to give a verdict. I can say, however, that it has the most enchanting light pink flowers, which have repeated well, that the glossy foliage looks as if it will be as good as that of 'Compassion' and that it is sending up new growth with the greatest abandon. I only wish it had a more attractive name. 'High Hopes' sounds like a nickname in the nursery and not something a fine rose should be saddled with all its life. Let us hope it does not restrict sales as unsuitable rose names have done in the past.

'Compassion' is probably the best climbing rose raised since the last war.

COMPLICATA

The lack of the traditional standards of morality in the genus *Rosa* has meant that all attempts at classification are doomed to failure. In the wild days of yore, different rose species coupled with an abandon that would have been envied even on Mount Olympus and no diaries were kept recording the liaisons; but man likes things to be orderly and many, many attempts have been made to sort out the muddle. There have been varying degrees of success but always, just when the going seemed smooth and straightforward, up popped a rose variety that did not fit anywhere or that seemed to slot half in one class and half in another. The latest valiant attempt on an international level to classify roses was made by The World Federation of Rose Societies and the main result for the average gardener was to change the floribundas to cluster-flowered bush roses and hybrid teas to large-flowered bush roses. This was supposed to clarify the situation, but old ways die hard and there has been resistance to a change for which the said average gardener could see no need. Resistance, too, came from nurserymen, those in the huge American market refusing to have anything to do with the new ruling, despite the fact that their own national society had endorsed the World Federation ideas.

Speaking for myself, as a council member of The Royal National Rose Society, which had not only endorsed the decision for change but had been largely instrumental in suggesting what changes should be made, I was extremely conscientious in using the new terms for many months. However, the more I tried, the more aware I became that the new system was far from providing an answer. The climax came when I had to describe a hybrid tea with flowers small for the type. Should I call it a small-flowered large-flowered rose? There was no sensible answer and I am afraid that I have reverted to the old ways.

All of which brings us to such varieties as 'Complicata' and 'Scarlet Fire' ('Scharlachglut'), both large, wide-ranging shrubs with long, arching shoots and for long described as gallicas, although the typical gallica is, as we have seen in the description of 'Charles de Mills', a fairly upright, twiggy shrub of only moderate size. 'Scarlet Fire' does seem to be a gallica hybrid, unlikely as it may seem from its appearance, since one of its parents was 'Alika' or *R. gallica* 'Grandiflora', brought from Russia in 1906 by

'Complicata' is not a rose grown for spectacular hips, but they can be attractive.

The huge, single, white-eyed flowers of 'Complicata' make a spectacular show in June.

N.E. Hansen. 'Complicata', on the other hand, has no such known link with any of the old families and strangely (for it is by no means a recent introduction) does not appear in any of the old books. It appears to be better known on the Continent than in the United Kingdom and research is going on at the present time in France as to its origins. The most likely theories are that it is either a canina or a macrantha hybrid, but if it is the latter we are not very much wiser as nobody knows for certain the origin of *R.* × *macrantha*. It is thought it may be of garden origin.

Despite all this, however, 'Complicata' is, like a mongrel dog, just as good as, and some say a good deal better than, many a rose of known breeding. It makes, as I said, a large shrub which, if given the chance, will ramble up and through even larger neighbours to a height of 10ft (3m) or more, covering them and itself in early summer with its great 5in (12cm), single, brilliant pink flowers which pale to white in the centre around a circle of golden-yellow stamens. They have been described as 'as large as saucers' and they will be so numerous that the foliage can vanish beneath them, though for most of the season it is an attractive feature in its own right: a rose that all who have the space should grow, bearing in mind that it is summer flowering only. In full bloom, it positively glows in bright sunlight.

The name 'Complicata' is just as puzzling as the rose's ancestry. There was some correspondence about this in the *Bulletin of the Historic Roses Group* of The Royal National Rose Society and an extract from a letter from Dr Aidan Daniel reads as follows: 'Complicated it certainly is not – a charming, simple bloom on a good grower. But "complicated" is a late development of the Latin word, which comes from "plicare", meaning to fold or pleat; hence the English words "plicated" and "plication", meaning "folded" or "pleated". Could the term have been applied to the rose because of the little folds or creases in the edge of the petals?' Peter Harkness, writing in his *The Photographic Encyclopedia of Roses*, agrees, and I think that we must accept this until information surfaces that will tell us we are wrong. Perhaps it will come via the French research into the history and lineage of this beautiful rose. We can but wait and see.

Comte De Chambord

At much the same time as the bourbon roses appeared on the scene, another and not dissimilar group was being developed, possibly in Italy. The original rose of this family was known as 'Paestana', taken from the Italian town of Paestum, a centre of rose propagation for the insatiable Roman market – for which roses were even grown under glass to lengthen the season when blooms would be available. It was also known rather later as the Scarlet Four Seasons Rose because, like the Autumn Damask, it flowered late as well as early, but the blooms of 'Paestana' much more closely resemble those of a gallica than they do a damask. It is now thought likely that this rose was the result of a China rose–gallica cross, and its upright stance is certainly that of a gallica. Altogether it has quite a resemblance to the gallica 'Officinalis', though the red colouring is brighter, verging on scarlet. The blooms open wide and flat to reveal golden stamens.

In most published accounts it is said that 'Paestana' was in England early in the nineteenth century, brought over from Italy by the third Duchess of Portland, and that from her it reached Dupont's nursery in Paris in 1809. It was he who named it 'Duchess of Portland' and it became the founder of the Portland rose line – though many people continued for some time to refer to it as a damask perpetual in reference to its long and comparatively continuous flowering period.

This has been the accepted story until recent research, described fully in Peter Beales's *Roses*, has indicated that the rose was more probably named after the second duchess than the third. Her dates were 1715–85, she was a keen rosarian and, since she never left England in her life, there must be some doubt that she brought the rose from Italy in the first place. It may be added in support of these suggested earlier dates that the rose was listed in a nursery catalogue of 1782. Redouté pictured it under the title *Le Rosier de Portland* but nowadays it is generally known in the United Kingdom as the Portland Rose and in the United States as 'Duchess of Portland'.

OPPOSITE: *The later Portland roses all had double flowers. This is pink, scented 'Comte de Chambord'.*

The original Portland rose, shown here, was also known as The Scarlet Four Seasons Rose.

*Like 'Comte de Chambord', 'Jacques Cartier' is an old rose
that is recurrent flowering.*

But what has all this to do with 'Comte de Chambord' which, in contrast to the rose we have so far been discussing, has large, pink, very double flowers? Well, it is a Portland rose and all the later varieties did have double flowers.

Apart from this, however, it is difficult to trace any real pattern in their development, which was largely eclipsed by that of their contemporaries, the bourbons, which had the combined resources of the French nursery trade solidly behind them. It has been said, in addition, that the Portlands are not easy to breed from but, whatever the reason, they never made very much of a mark. Reading through books of the period, to find a mention of them is rare and it is only in the quite recent past that their qualities

have at last come to be recognized. The bourbons, of course, have their own place in the scheme of things, but if a rose of a similar type is needed for a small garden or indeed for a small space, one that is almost perpetually in flower right through to the autumn, then a Portland rose is the one to choose.

'Comte de Chambord' is probably the most widely grown Portland rose today. It was introduced in 1860 (raiser and parentage unknown but I wonder if one parent was a bourbon) and is a real beauty. In habit of growth it does resemble 'Duchess of Portland', in that it is busy and upright and, perhaps most typical of all, it has a characteristic shared by many of the other Portlands. This is what Graham Thomas has graphically called 'a high-shouldered effect, with the topmost leaves forming a "collar" round each open bloom', and the plant is generally well covered with its rather pointed light green foliage. The flowers, however, which are larger than those of any other Portland, are completely different from those of 'Duchess of Portland', being of a clear rose-pink, very double and sometimes quartered. They are very fragrant and carried almost continuously from June until the autumn in moderate-sized clusters at the top of the bush, although the weight of the clusters may cause the outer shoots to arch outward. It will grow to about 4ft (1.2m) in height and, for such a double rose, the weather resistance is surprisingly good.

The second most popular Portland – not, I think, quite as good as 'Comte de Chambord' – is 'Jacques Cartier'. The flowers are rather smaller, opening cupped with a button eye, and are of a brighter pink. Once again it makes a compact, upright shrub. Other Portlands to look out for are blush-pink to white 'Mabel Morrison', crimson 'Rose de Rescht', crimson-purple 'Arthur de Sensal', pink 'Mme Knorr' and 'Rose du Roi'. The last was raised in 1815 by Comte Lelieur who, as superintendent of the Imperial Gardens in France, was one of those who saw the potential of this rose group and played quite a part in keeping it going and developing it.

Constance Spry

Breeding a new rose variety is a long process, needing great patience and perseverance. From the time of choosing prospective parent varieties and cross pollinating them, to the launch of the final variety on the market, can easily take eight years. First there is the gathering and sowing of the seed from the hips and then the long period while the resultant seedlings are growing and decisions being made as to whether they are likely to develop into anything worthwhile. Few of them will, but those that show promise will be persevered with for another season or two until eventually grafted plants from a final selection may be sent for trials. These are likely to take place in several countries and certainly in as many nurseries as possible in the country where they were raised. When reports start coming back after a year or so, it may then be decided that one or two of the roses justify being put on the market. It is no use, however, launching a new rose if you only have half a dozen – or even half a hundred – plants. You need thousands, and this sort of quantity will take probably two years to build up.

It is a long, long road, but it can be said that it is not unduly difficult to breed a good (as opposed to an outstanding) floribunda and perhaps that little bit harder to find a good hybrid tea. Cross two existing varieties and, with luck, something reasonable will come out, but you are not really creating anything new. It will simply be a variation on what has gone before and, quite frankly, there are far too many roses like that.

It is when original thinking comes into the process of hybridizing, such as the introduction of the genes of a so far untried wild rose, that things become more complicated. A whole new stage is introduced into the sequence, for crossing a once-flowering species with a recurrent variety does not, in the first generation, produce another recurrent rose. It may take a generation or two before things stabilize into a recurrent pattern and, for a hybridist who is also a nurseryman and is dependent on selling what he produces to make a living, it takes courage

Although 'Constance Spry' is quite a modern rose, its blooms are in the old rose style.

*'Constance Spry' was the first step in David Austin's
English Rose breeding programme.*

There have been others who have been prepared to experiment and take a chance with something new, and no one has been more successful in this than Albrighton nurseryman David Austin. He has not primarily experimented with species but conceived the idea of crossing old, once-flowering roses with modern varieties to combine the best of both – the sumptuous, many-petalled blooms of the roses of the last century with the recurrent-flowering habit possessed by roses today. He began experimenting on these lines in the late 1950s and in an exceedingly short time in terms of rose breeding came up with a winner. This was a cross between the extremely beautiful pink Le Grice floribunda 'Dainty Maid' and the blush-pink gallica 'Belle Isis' of 1845, which produced a rose utterly unlike either of them. I am referring, of course, to 'Constance Spry' which he introduced in 1961.

Although a magnificient rose, it was not recurrent and so only a step towards what David Austin had set out to achieve. Nevertheless, because of the glorious, many-petalled flowers, more sumptuous, I would say, than any of the true old roses, and its terrific constitution, it has been accepted for what it is and not what it might have been. The blooms are fragrant, likened to the scent of myrrh, though not in my experience as strongly scented as has been claimed, and are carried with great freedom. They are a pleasing pink and the petals reflex gradually as the blooms open. Left to its own devices, 'Constance Spry' will make a huge, sprawling shrub, which is best with the support of a large tripod, round which its shoots can be spiralled. Otherwise it can be grown as a climber on a wall, when it will go up to about 15ft (4.5m). A quite stunning rose all round but do remember that it is a variety that must have (and insists on having) its head. It really cannot do itself justice in a confined space.

'Constance Spry' has been the foundation on which David Austin has built. When we come to describe such varieties as 'Graham Thomas' the story will be taken a stage further, but its end is by no means yet in sight.

OPPOSITE: *So vigorous is it that 'Constance Spry' needs the
support of a frame of some kind.*

to tread such a little-explored path. Credit must be given to Sam McGredy for deciding to 'boldly go where no man had gone before' with his floribunda 'Maxi' of 1971, which had *R. macrophylla* 'Coryana' in its pedigree. Its family tree, believe it or not, read ['Evelyn Fison' × ('Tantau's Triumph' × *R. macrophylla* 'Coryana')] × ('Hamburger Phoenix' × 'Danse du Feu'). 'Maxi' played an important part in the McGredy 'hand-painted' line of roses through 'Priscilla Burton' and introduced something new in the way of flower colour patternings. Very much later, Jack Harkness and Alex Cocker of Aberdeen joined forces in experimenting with the very un-rose-like *R. persica*, pictured by Redouté under the name *R. berberifolia*. This had yellow, dark-centred flowers more resembling those of a halimium than a rose and from it came varieties such as 'Euphrates' and 'Nigel Hawthorne'. These, though of great interest, have not, and are scarcely likely to, set the rose world on fire unless someone can be found to carry on their development.

DAINTY BESS

There can be no flower more beautiful, I think, than the fully expanded bloom of 'Dainty Bess'; but then, I have probably said just the same thing about the individual flowers of such varieties as 'Frühlingsmorgen' or 'Ellen Willmott' and quite a number of other single beauties. Still, that is the way it always goes and one is probably influenced in one's judgement by the mood of the moment. I refuse, however, to believe that this is so with 'Dainty Bess'. Regardless of mood, it is always supremely beautiful.

It is, surprisingly, a hybrid tea, surprisingly because its fragrant flowers have only five large petals of a silky, light pink set off to perfection by the crown of purple stamens in the centre. It makes an exceptionally free-flowering, vigorous bush, growing to about 3ft (1m), with dark, leathery foliage. It was raised in 1925 by W.E.B. Archer & Daughter of Sellinge, near Hythe in Kent, from a cross between 'Ophelia', from which it must have got its delicate colouring, and the brilliant scarlet-crimson 'K of K'.

'Dainty Bess' won a well-deserved National Rose Society Gold Medal in its year of introduction, though in those days roses were not put through a rigorous three-year trial period as they are today. They were judged on their showing when exhibited at the Rose Society's Autumn Show, which meant really on their performance on one particular day, so that a good deal of luck inevitably was involved. There are trials even today, particularly on the Continent, that are still conducted in the same way – which fact should be taken into account when assessing their value – but it can be said with confidence that with 'Dainty Bess' the award was well earned. If confirmation of this were needed, it gained an RHS Award of Merit in the same year, although surprisingly it has not retained it in the latest (1994) revised list of awards to roses. As one of the advisers to the RHS Floral 'A' Committee that makes these awards, I intend to try to put this right. The National Rose Society Annual of 1926 described it as a 'first rate decorative rose that will be in large demand by the exhibitors in the ladies' Artistic Rose Sections'.

'Dainty Bess' was not the only single hybrid tea put out by the Archer family, for in 1936 they introduced 'Ellen Willmott' from a cross between 'Dainty Bess' and 'Lady Hillingdon'. This has the same large-petalled flowers in a creamy-lemon colour, flushed rosy-pink, and grows into a large, upright bush. The lovely soft orange tints of 'Lady Hillingdon' were not, in this case, passed on and for a single-flowered hybrid tea in approximately that colour range one has to go back to 1921, when the Essex firm of Cant brought out 'Mrs Oakley Fisher'. In this the large clusters are a buff-orange, unshaded, with pronounced amber stamens and bronzy, dark green leaves carried on a bush with plum-red stems. It will grow to 2ft (60cm) on average, but I have seen it considerably taller, reaching, in fact, about 5ft (1.5m) and 3–4ft (1–1.2m) across. It is of open, airy habit and it is worth recording that this one gained an RHS Award of Merit in 1921.

OPPOSITE: *It comes as a surprise to many that there are hybrid teas with single, five-petalled flowers. 'Dainty Bess' is among the most beautiful of them.*

'Mrs Oakley Fisher', a single hybrid tea,
was raised in 1921.

'Ellen Willmott' was an offspring of 'Dainty Bess', from the
same Kent nursery.

Although 'Mrs Oakley Fisher' goes back to 1921, it was by no means the first of the single hybrid teas. At the very beginning of the present century the Northern Irish breeder Alex Dickson produced a series of, I believe, seven varieties, ranging from creamy-white 'Irish Beauty' and 'Irish Modesty' of 1900 to tangerine 'Irish Afterglow' of 1918. In between came 'Irish Harmony' in very pale yellow and the strangely named 'Irish Engineer' (rose-pink) both of 1904, followed by 'Irish Elegance' with large, orange-scarlet blooms, shaded bronze, and with good foliage and vigorous, upright growth.

With the latter rose the Dickson single hybrid teas really began to be noticed, for although the earlier 'Irish Harmony' had gained a Gold Medal in 1904, it did not make a great impression on the public. A second Gold Medal winner, 'Irish Fireflame', introduced in 1914, did, however, make a considerable impact with its lovely crimson-splashed buds opening to fragrant blooms of orange to old-gold, veined crimson, and with light, fawn-coloured anthers. The foliage was (and still is) dark and glossy and the rose makes a sturdy bush. There is a climbing form of 'Irish Fireflame' as well.

Anyone who has not grown one of these single hybrid teas is not among the blessed, but this can soon be rectified as a number of them can be obtained from specialist nurseries. As far as I can trace, 'Irish Fireflame' and 'Irish Elegance' are the only two of the Dickson roses to have survived, along with Archer's 'Dainty Bess' and 'Ellen Willmott' plus 'Mrs Oakley Fisher' and yet one more, the Gold Medal-winning light rose-pink 'Isobel' from Sam McGredy. The other Irish roses may still be growing somewhere in monkish solitude in a forgotten garden, but they have for long been out of commerce. Give these wonderful varieties a go. Start with 'Dainty Bess' and take it from there.

DUPONTII

Though considered to be a cross between R. *gallica* and R. *moschata* and so not a true wild rose, R. × *dupontii* has all the attributes of a species – tall, arching growth, the long shoots carrying clusters of single flowers. The blooms are, in fact, larger than those of most species, reaching probably 3in (8cm) across, and open to a creamy white with a slight pink blush which, however, soon fades. The stamens are pale yellow and the petals are rounded and so broad that they overlap one another and give the impression that this is a semi-double rather than a single rose. Sweetly fragrant, the blooms are carried all over the bush, both high up and low down, and of course in between. It is a tall grower, reaching 7ft (2.1m) or so and as much across, with shoots that stay green and have few prickles. The leaves are a soft grey-green and disease free, blending happily with other shrubs in a mixed planting. New growth comes freely from the base, which suggests that the complete removal of one or two shoots each year could be carried out with advantage.

The history of this rose is interesting in that it is said to have been raised some time prior to 1817 by M. Dupont, who was the founder of the Luxembourg rose garden, Paris, and who helped the Empress Josephine to assemble her rose collection at Malmaison. Redouté probably painted it there, for it appears in Vol I, Plate 63, of his *Les Roses*, though under the name R. *damascene subalba*. A bit of a puzzle this, for M. Dupont called it *Rosa nivea*. The name R. × *dupontii* was finally given to it by Lindley in 1825.

That, however, is not the only uncertainty about this rose. R. × *dupontii* is, as has been said, supposed to be a cross between R. × *gallica* and R. *moschata* and, if this was a deliberate mating of two roses by M. Dupont, it must have been one of the earliest cases of planned hybridization of which there is a record. But the puzzle that baffled growers and botanists alike for many years, until Graham Thomas put his mind to sorting it out, was this: what exactly was R. *moschata* (the musk rose)? Drawing on his encyclopaedic knowledge of the rose and rose history, he began to delve.

The initial trouble was that in the old days virtually every single, white-flowered rose was known as a musk rose. However, since many of these flowered early in the year and the old herbals all concurred in saying that the musk rose bloomed late, from August onward, this clearly could not be right. Shakespeare's lines from *A Midsummer Night's Dream*: 'with sweet musk roses and with eglantine' almost certainly refer to R. *arvensis* or the Field Rose, the only white rose to grow wild in the UK, which has already been referred to on page 8.

The situation was not helped by the adoption of the name musk rose for the ultra-vigorous, white-flowered climbers and ramblers from the Far East. Many of these were actually forms or hybrids of R. *brunonii* and nothing at all to do with the musk rose, and how this transfer of the name to a completely different family came about is not known. John Gerard, in his *Herball* of 1597 says, 'the musk rose flowereth in Autumn, or the fall of the leaf; the rest flower when the Damask and the red rose do', which certainly does not fit varieties like R. *brunonii* 'La Mortola' or 'Paul's Himalayan Musk Rambler'.

Although a hybrid, 'Dupontii' has the single flowers and arching growth of a species.

There is not space here to follow the tortuous path that Graham Thomas was forced to take in his quest for the true musk rose. The amount of conflicting evidence would have daunted a lesser man. Those who would like to learn more can do no better than to read Graham's own account in his book *Climbing Roses Old and New*, but perhaps I might be allowed to quote from the climax to his story. 'Almost the last book I looked at,' he writes, 'was *My Garden in Summer* by E.A. Bowles, 1914. Here I found: "The true and rare old musk rose exists here, but in a juvenile state at present, for it is not many years since I brought it as a cutting from the splendid old specimen on the Grange at Bitton, and I must not expect its deliciously scented, late-in-the-season flowers before it has scrambled up its wall space." The Grange, Bitton, was Canon Ellacombe's home.

'Dupontii' was probably raised at Malmaison, near Paris.

'Through the kindness of Mr W.G. MacKenzie, who, together with the curatorship of the Chelsea Physic Garden combines the chairmanship of the committee caring for Mr Bowles's garden, now an outlying part of London University, I visited Myddelton House in late August 1963. And there, on a cold north-west facing wall of the house was a rose just coming into flower. It was without doubt the Old Musk Rose. I had walked straight to it.'

And so what was this mysterious rose really like? Said to come variously from Madeira, North Africa, Spain and Southern Europe to Western Asia, it forms a 12ft (3.5m) arching, freely branching bush with oval, glabrous leaves and creamy-white single flowers in late summer, carrying on into the autumn. It is, of course, strongly scented. I am aware that this description could equally well fit any number of wild roses, but it is the best I can do. Those dissatisfied must try to see it for themselves.

ELINA

This name may not immediately ring a bell as the rose which bears it was introduced in 1985 by the Dickson Nurseries of Northern Ireland as 'Peaudouce'. In fact it was chosen strictly for business reasons, for nurseries, just like any other business, have to make a profit to survive. It is part of their good fortune that they make their money by producing something beautiful, but there is, of course, no guarantee that every new rose they put on the market will catch on with the public. They have, if they can, to acquire what might be called 'bankers', and one way of doing this is to find a sponsor for certain varieties.

Healthy, robust and always in flower, 'Elina' is one of the finest roses of modern times.

A number of companies, often completely unconnected with the world of horticulture, will pay sums running into four figures – if not five – to have a rose named after them or one of their products. It is a publicity exercise, of course, which achieves its purpose by the repeated exposure of the company's name every time the rose is mentioned, in print or at the point of sale. Examples of roses apart from 'Peaudouce' that have been named in this way are 'Benson and Hedges Gold' after a cigarette, 'Arthur Bell' and 'Glenfiddich' after whisky brands, 'Bonsoir' after a make of pyjamas, the 'Daily Mail Rose' and 'Liverpool Echo' after newspapers, 'Radox Bouquet' after a bath salt and 'Savoy Hotel'. 'Peaudouce' was named after a brand of children's nappy, and I suppose that, if one forgot the commercial aspect and thought only of the literal translation of the French *peaudouce*, which is 'smooth' or 'soft skin', there could be worse names for a rose – just. And I know that at the time of its launch there were those who felt that Pat Dickson, its raiser, had perhaps been not too wise in linking one of the best roses he had ever produced with a product bearing such unromantic connotations. Be that as it may, it is now clear that the licence granted to the Peaudouce company was of only a limited duration, and one might say that wisdom has prevailed. The rose is now called 'Elina', and it is to be hoped that the confusion caused by the change of name will not affect the sales of this outstanding variety.

There are people who think that 'Elina', with its huge, pale, creamy-yellow blooms, which have a deeper tone at the heart of the flower, may be the

The blooms of 'Elina' are always carried one to a stem and are always immaculate.

long-awaited rival to 'Peace'. The vigour of both is about the same, for both will top 4ft (1.2m), which is not surprising if one looks back through 'Elina's family tree. The immediate parents were 'Nana Mouskouri' × 'Lolita', and 'Karl Herbst', which came directly from a 'Peace' cross that appears in both their pedigrees a few generations back. The pale, creamy yellow of the blooms of 'Elina' is not unlike that of 'Peace', though lacking the pink flushes of the latter. However, 'Elina's flowers are more classical in shape, with their high, pointed centres and, because of this, they are much more suitable for exhibition purposes. They are always carried one to a stem and never in clusters, and it is difficult to think of another rose with flowers of a comparable size that is so continuously in bloom. As with 'Peace', the scent is only moderate.

Where 'Elina' differs most from 'Peace' is in its foliage. That of the latter has a fine gloss and a general suggestion of robust health. The leaves of 'Elina' are dark green and handsome too, but they are only semi-glossy and may develop mildew in the second half of the season. This is something that became evident in my garden only after having grown 'Elina' for about four years. Previously to that the foliage had been almost completely disease free and one can but hope that this rose is not following in the steps of 'Super Star', which started off equally well but deteriorated in health very quickly. But that is to take, probably, a far too pessimistic view.

It is much too early to say whether 'Elina' will still be going strong after fifty years, which is something 'Peace' has achieved; and meanwhile, with a little help from a good fungicide from July onwards, 'Elina' is one of the most beautiful and rewarding roses that you can grow. It is long lasting in a vase and long lasting in the garden.

Escapade

There is no floribunda, in all the years I have been growing them, that has performed better than 'Escapade'. It is early into flower in June, quick to repeat so that there are few years when there are less than three flushes of bloom, and it carries large heads of white-centred flowers of a rosy-violet unique among roses. The foliage is a light, bright green right from the time when the leaves unfurl, for it is one of those roses which miss out on the usual early red tints, making it stand out in the garden long before the flower buds open. The plant breaks freely from the base and grows to about 3ft (1m) in height.

Its raiser, the late Jack Harkness, always considered 'Escapade' his finest rose.

It is healthy and the flowers seem just as happy in a vase as they do in the garden. Cut them before they are fully expanded to obtain the richest colour.

The parents of 'Escapade' were 'Pink Parfait' × 'Baby Faurax', the latter a polyantha with small amethyst blooms, and among that strange band of roses that keeps appearing in the pedigrees of other roses but which is never actually seen growing in a garden. 'Floradora' (pollen parent of 'Queen Elizabeth') is one and 'Cläre Grammerstorf', from which 'Honeymoon', 'Arthur Bell' and 'Chinatown' derive, is another. 'Rudolph Timm' is a third example, and from this variety came 'Margaret Merril' and 'Saga'. A discerning hybridist will, time and again, see qualities they are looking for in the most unlikely roses, and in a big rose-breeding programme many varieties may never get beyond the seedling stage and yet be used in crosses with others to pass on certain desirable qualities.

With so much going for it, why is 'Escapade' not more widely grown? Unfortunately, the answer seems to be that it is not a 'saleable' colour. There are certain hues that only a minority of buyers go for and most of the pale and pastel shades come into this category. So do white roses, although the one outstanding exception to this is 'Iceberg', which is seen in more gardens than almost any other rose. Its sheer exuberance wins people over, but the same has not happened to the equally good 'Escapade'. It is to be hoped that the fact that the old garden roses are gaining in popularity all the time, and that 'Escapade' will blend most happily with them, may help to change things in time.

The late Jack Harkness was the raiser of 'Escapade' and it was his first real success as a breeder. He was enormously successful right from the start and in 1964 began to select the first results of his work for introduction. In his estimation the best of these was 'Escapade' (which has now been voted an Award of Merit by the RHS), though other early ones were more popular, probably because they were more conventional. They included 'King Arthur', 'Guinevere', 'Sir Lancelot' and 'Merlin', all of which came out in 1967. The only one of these I grew was 'Sir Lancelot', which was a very pleasing orange colour, but also prone to black spot. Since that time great emphasis has been placed by the Harkness breeding establishment on producing disease-resistant roses, and among their outstanding introductions are 'Alexander', the climber 'Compassion', 'Mountbatten', 'Yesterday', 'Elizabeth Harkness', 'Southampton', 'Amber Queen' and 'Margaret Merril'. The more adventurous side of the programme produced some novelties such as the strange-coloured 'Greensleeves' and 'Cosette' with its unusual petal formation. Probably the healthiest rose in my garden (except for the unmatched rugosas) is the Harkness yellow floribunda 'Princess Michael of Kent' which has flowers almost of hybrid tea size and would probably be more widely stocked by nurseries if it were a more even grower.

The blooms of 'Escapade' are of a rosy-violet unmatched by any other rose.

FANTIN-LATOUR

Frequently the question is asked: 'What is your favourite rose?'. The accepted reply to such an impossible question is: 'The last one I looked at', but how can you pick a favourite from a family, the tallest member of which might grow to 40ft (12m), the smallest to 6in (15cm), that has enchanting five-petalled single flowers and great blowsy ones of about one hundred petals, and that can come in all colours of the rainbow with the exception of blue? It cannot be done, but I can say with certainty that 'Fantin-Latour' would have an honoured place on my short-list.

The flowers, carried in clusters, are quite enchanting. Of the softest blush-pink, with more richly tinted centre petals, they open to a circular, cupped shape. The outer petals then reflex, leaving the centre cupped, and at that stage it can scarcely be surpassed for beauty. So freely are they borne that at peak flowering time some of the more slender branches of what is in general a sturdy and upright 5–6ft (1.5–1.8m) bush can become borne down with their weight. This is a habit generally recognized as being typical of a member of the centifolia family, and it is with the centifolias that 'Fantin-Latour' is generally grouped. The evidence is, however, rather scant, for no one has the least idea where or when it originated, except that it was probably during the lifetime of the French artist after whom it was named.

Normally one would grow 'Fantin-Latour' as a free-standing shrub, perhaps as a specimen or in a collection of other old roses, but the New Zealand grower, the late Nancy Steen, had it planted next to a *Cotinus coggygria*, the Smoke Bush, through which it

'Fantin-Latour' is a centifolia, a family seen in many of the old Dutch flower paintings.

chose to ramble, the flowers festooning the dark branches of the *Cotinus*. Many of the old roses will ramble in this way if provided with something in which really to express themselves, and with many centifolias the support of another shrub or some kind of frame is necessary. They can be rather lax, ungainly growers with their lovely blooms weighed right to the ground at flowering time if not appropriately held up. 'Fantin-Latour', however, is satisfyingly self-supporting in most situations.

There is some confusion about the name centifolia, first of all because it means, literally, one hundred leaves. This particular point is easily cleared

'Fantin-Latour' is here seen in The Gardens of the Rose near St Albans in Hertfordshire.

up, as in the old herbals, including that of John Gerard, 'folia' is used for both leaves and petals in flower descriptions. It is less easy to give a definite answer to a second question.

The old Roman writers (Pliny and Co.) refer to centifolia roses, but it seems likely that they were simply indicating that a rose had many petals rather than referring to a specific number or a specific kind. Research seems to indicate that the centifolias we know originated somewhere in eastern Europe with both damask and alba blood in them and first appeared in Holland in the sixteenth century. Here they were steadily developed over the next century or so, largely by careful selection, for as a race they are largely sterile. On the other hand, they throw out bud-sports with considerable freedom and it was these that the Dutch breeders concentrated on until the group expanded enough to become widely known as Holland roses. Gradually, however, the French began to take an ever greater hand in their development, particularly in the south, and the name changed, according to Parkinson in his *Paradisus* of 1629, to 'The great double Damask Province' rose.

This led in due course to confusion with the gallica (French) rose, known with much better reason as the Rose of Provins, for it was round the town of Provins near Paris that it was grown commercially in large quantities. To sort out the muddle, the centifolia became instead the Provence Rose, which name it still bears today. It is also known as the Cabbage Rose.

All of which may or may not be relevant to 'Fantin-Latour' because, as I said at the beginning, it is by no means certain that it is really a centifolia. However, treat it as if it were one and you will not go far wrong. Being once-flowering in June and early July, any pruning should be carried out after flowering, cutting back long main shoots by about one-quarter and shortening side shoots by two-thirds. A number of people – those who never prune old roses – do not bother even to do this, but in my experience it does produce more flowers the following summer. It may be necessary to spray the large, handsome, dark green leaves against mildew in late summer, but one application should be enough to keep them clear for the rest of the season.

FELICIA

The Reverend Joseph Pemberton, who raised the hybrid musk group of roses, has already been mentioned briefly when discussing the rose 'Ballerina'. Some doubt was expressed that 'Ballerina' was really one of the family, as it was launched well after the death of Pemberton, but there can be no doubt about 'Felicia', which, coming fairly late in the hybrid musk story, is considered by many people to be the peak of Pemberton's achievement. Like 'Ballerina', it was not actually introduced during his lifetime, as it did not appear until 1928 and he died in 1926. However, he had been partnered in his nursery and breeding programme by his sister Florence, who was to carry on for some time alone. 'Felicia' was well and truly launched before she, too, died in 1929 and there is little doubt that Pemberton himself was the man who raised it.

Those who do not already know the story may wonder what a clergyman was doing running a very successful nursery, but it really came about by chance. The introduction to the Pemberton's *Select Rose List* of 1916, which I have before me as I write, gives the explanation. 'The Roses offered in this List', it says, 'are Dwarf or Bush Plants. They have been grown and cultivated by the Rev. Joseph Pemberton and Miss Florence Pemberton primarily for their own enjoyment. Friends, however, have desired plants, so the Roses are now offered to the general public.' In other words the Pembertons, who had been highly successful growers and also exhibitors of roses as a hobby, suddenly found themselves almost forced to become nurserymen to fulfil the requests of their friends.

The link between hybrid musks and the true musk rose is tenuous, to say the least. If there is one at all, it must come through R. *multiflora*, which has some affinity with it, and was one parent of Peter Lambert's 'Trier'. This was raised in 1904 as a shrub rose of very satisfactory growth habit, which must have prompted Pemberton to use it to try to improve on the ungainly and leggy hybrid perpetuals which were the popular garden roses of the time. He succeeded probably beyond his wildest dreams, not really in producing replacements for the perpetuals but in creating a group of roses that could stand on its own through sheer merit. How the group became known as hybrid musks has already been told, but in

'Felicia' is one of the hybrid musk group of roses raised by the Rev. Joseph Pemberton.

fact they are such a mixed bag that by the time 'Prosperity' came along in 1919 and 'Vanity' in 1920, the original 'Trier' line had all but vanished. Hybrid teas and other roses had been introduced into the pedigrees and all that they retained in common was their ability to make attractive, freely branching shrubs which flowered well and had a good autumn repeat. Quite enough, too, most people would say, but not enough to make them botanically a family.

'Felicia' is one of the group which, although coming fairly late in the sequence, did retain 'Trier' as a parent, the other parent being that classic hybrid tea 'Ophelia'. David Austin writes that the flowers retain something of the latter rose's qualities but, apart from the fact that both are pink, I cannot see it myself. They come in large clusters, first as rather pointed, apricot-pink buds and then open out into informal, blush-pink, double flowers which have strong fragrance. The glossy leaves certainly lean toward those of a hybrid tea, being broader and of more substance than those of a typical hybrid musk. They are healthy and are carried on a strong, freely branching bush which will grow up to about 5ft (1.5m) in height. The first flush of bloom will be in late May, lasting for several weeks, with another flush, often equally good, in September.

'Felicia' is an excellent rose for specimen planting or it will mix very happily with other shrubs, including other shrub roses. It can also make an excellent hedge planted, free-standing, about 4ft (1.2m) apart if you have room, or else trained on horizontal wires or, better still, on a chain-link fence if your space is somewhat limited.

There is a saying that it does not matter what colour hybrid musks start out; they all end up white. This is true up to a point and some of them certainly do fade when the sun shines, but 'Felicia' is one that does hold its colour very well.

This picture shows what a colourful hedge 'Felicia' will make if trained on a support.

FRAGRANT CLOUD

Back in the days when the three Mattock brothers were still running their nursery near Oxford, I remember John telling me that customers would come in and tell him that they wanted only those roses that were scented; what would he advise? Sent out to the rose fields to make their choice, the customers would come back with a list of varieties, perhaps only fifty per cent of which had any noticeable fragrance. It was the colour of the blooms that had influenced their choice, which, when you think about it, makes sense. There are comparatively few roses, other than the synstile group of ramblers, which release their fragrance freely into the air. With most you have to bend close to catch the scent, and what percentage of the average person's time in the

'Fragrant Cloud' is one of the sweetest scented of all roses.

garden is spent in sniffing? Much more, I think, on looking and admiring, if not from afar at least from some distance away. The colour is still there to be seen, wherever you stand.

Rather a prosaic way of looking at things? Perhaps, but practical. However, to appreciate flowers to the full there should ideally be an appeal to all the senses; and a rose is expected, by tradition if not from actual experience, to be scented. Which brings me to 'Fragrant Cloud', one of the most sweet-smelling roses of modern times. It was introduced in 1963 by Matthias Tantau, a German hybridist who only rarely reveals the parentage of any of the roses he has raised. This time he did give the information that it was a Seedling × 'Prima Ballerina', the latter a strongly scented rose which has been used in the breeding of a number of other good varieties but which, in my garden at least, rapidly became white with mildew each summer and ended up, finely shredded, on the compost heap.

Mildew, however, has never been a problem with the 'Fragrant Cloud' bushes I grow. There can be some black spot towards the end of the season and a number of people have told me they have found a greater tendency to this than there used to be. Disease, though, could hardly have been a major problem when the rose was introduced for it won the highest award in The Royal National Rose Society trials, a Gold Medal, topped up by the President's International Trophy, which signifies something really outstanding. Known as 'Duftwolke' in its native Germany and as 'Nuage Parfumé' in France, it makes a bushy plant with handsome, deep green

Such is the freedom of bloom of 'Fragrant Cloud' that it was first considered a floribunda.

foliage and very large, full, coral-red blooms which are borne with great freedom and are quick to repeat. As a bedding rose it can have few equals, and such a profuse flowerer is it that on its original introduction in Germany it was considered a floribunda.

How, then, does 'Fragrant Cloud' tie in with the oft-repeated statement that modern roses have lost their fragrance? The answer is, of course, that they have not. There are still as many scented varieties as ever there were. The Rose Society publication *Roses to Enjoy* lists seventy-five just like that, without claiming to be comprehensive. They include, taking only those names which begin with an 'A' or 'B' from the alphabetical list, 'Alec's Red', 'Alpine Sunset', 'Amber Queen', 'Apricot Nectar', 'Arthur Bell', 'Barkarole', 'Beauty Queen', 'Big Purple', 'Blue Parfum', 'Buccaneer' and 'Burma Star'. You have only to read a reliable grower's catalogue to find many more, so why should this belief have come about that modern roses have no scent?

In part, at least, it must be due to the phenomenal rise in the popularity of the floribunda since the last war. Their ability to flower almost without pause and their often bright and cheerful colours have caused their sales to soar at the expense of other roses, including hybrid teas, though the latter have held their own better in the United Kingdom than in many other countries. And the ancestral roses that went into the forming of the floribunda group – the polyanthas and others before them – were not noted for their scent. Thus many of the new floribundas inherited this trait and, because they were so widely grown, gave the impression that it applied to all new roses. Even with the floribundas, scent is now being bred back and three of the varieties in the random list quoted above come into this category.

However, there are many varieties from the last century, still grown today, that are lacking in fragrance and obviously there must have been many more that have long since vanished. I will call on Pliny's *Natural History* for evidence that not all old roses were fragrant. Writing *c.* AD65 he said: 'In other districts, too, the genuine rose also depends to a very great extent upon soil for its main characteristics. The rose of Cyrene has the finest perfume, for which reason the finest perfume is to be obtained from there. At Carthage in Spain [sic] there is an early rose that blooms throughout the winter. Weather too makes a difference; for in certain years the rose grows with less perfume, and furthermore all roses have more perfume on dry soils than moist.' A long way from Pliny to 'Fragrant Cloud', but I grow mine, perforce, on very dry soil, so he obviously knew what he was talking about.

FRU DAGMAR HASTRUP

First a word about the name of this rose, as it has been the subject of some confusion. It has, for many years, gone under two names, the most commonly used being 'Frau Dagmar Hartopp'. Where this other name originated I have not been able to find out, but the alternative 'Fru Dagmar Hastrup' seems more likely to be the right one as the rose was raised in the Hastrup Nurseries in Denmark (in 1914) and Fru is the Danish equivalent of the German Frau.

The name established, what of the family, the rugosas? *R. rugosa*, the species from which all rugosas are descended, is a native of China and Japan and was introduced to the West round about 1840. It makes a

The rugosa family, to which 'Fru Dagmar Hastrup' belongs, is noted for its fine hips.

rather ungainly plant with flowers of a not particularly pleasing magenta-purple and is generally not considered as a worthy garden plant. However, this does not prevent certain nurseries selling it, or something very close to the original, as a cheap-offer hedging shrub.

Jack Harkness has written in *Roses*: 'A peculiar difficulty in breeding with *R. rugosa* is that the species and the types similar to it are in a great haste to shed their pollen ... By the time the buds were large enough to handle, the pollen was already being ejected. We therefore used rugosas as pollen parents, not for seed, but obtained little from them, in common with nearly all other breeders. On being mated with other roses their sterling qualities vanished with the first generation and I never succeeded in recalling their health and vigour subsequently. We badly need their health, and to know why they resist mildew, black spot and rust so efficiently.' He might have added that they also appear to resist the attentions of aphids or greenfly, which, as most gardeners know, are so prolific because they not only hatch out from eggs but also, like traffic cones, give birth to live young.

I have brought up the question of breeding with the rugosas as virtually all those we grow in our gardens today, including 'Fru Dagmar Hastrup', are hybrids raised around the turn of the century; so somebody has managed to do something with them and produce some first-rate shrubs in the process. Almost all retain the deeply veined or rugose foliage of the original and its extreme thorniness, so that they make admirable intruder-proof hedges. The

'Fru Dagmar Hastrup' makes an ideal small garden rose at 4ft (1.2m) in height.

fact that they were raised in comparatively recent times has led to their classification as modern shrub roses, but despite this they have for long been much more associated with the old roses. It is rare to find an old rose collection that does not include rugosa varieties.

'Fru Dagmar Hastrup' is one of the most beautiful of the rugosas with large, soft pink, single flowers with creamy-yellow stamens and a sweet fragrance. The blooms have no trace of the magenta that is usually found in the flowers of this family except, of course, the white and yellow ones. It is vigorous but is, nevertheless, one of the shorter rugosas, rarely topping 4ft (1.2m). It makes a good, low hedge and is a great favourite with local authorities for mass planting in parks and by roadsides, being practically trouble free.

After a first flush in June there will always be some flowers in the interval before the second flush appears. They are carried in small clusters and are followed by rounded hips like large radishes, but deep red rather than pink. Although 'Fru Dagmar Hastrup' is thought by some to be a seedling of *R. rugosa*, it germinates easily and usually the seeds come true, which makes this derivation rather unlikely. Hips begin to form after the first flowers fade so that they and the later blooms will be on the bush at the same time. Some dead-heading will increase later flower production, but you will get plenty of autumn bloom even if this is not carried out.

The rugosas are noted for their hips as well as for their other good qualities, but when making a choice of varieties it should be remembered that it is only the single and some semi-double varieties, such as 'Fru Dagmar Hastrup', rugosa 'Alba' and rugosa 'Rubra' and 'Scabrosa', that bear them. The Grootendorst varieties and such roses as 'Blanc Double de Coubert' do not. With the latter they raise hopes by starting to form, but they never change colour and ripen, and soon drop off.

R. Glauca
(R. Rubrifolia)

Here is a case where a change in the name of a rose has been brought about by the rules of horticultural nomenclature. Whether these rules should be followed is another matter, especially when a long-established and familiar name is discarded, and this is apparently something that is receiving serious consideration. The ultimate absurdity was the abandoning of the name chrysanthemum in favour of dendranthema, and quite rightly many nurseries have refused to co-operate. So far as one can tell the story of the change from *R. rubrifolia* went something like this.

'The name *R. rubrifolia*, given to the rose in 1789, was found to be antedated by that given it in 1788, which was *R. glauca*. However, it is argued that *R. glauca* should be discarded as it had already been widely used for yet another rose in the canina family. If this were done, however, it would be impossible to go back to *R. rubrifolia* which Villars rendered illegitimate by citing his own earlier named species *R. ferugiea* as a synonym, though it is believed that the two were not, in fact, the same, since the leaves were different. The illegitimacy of the name *R. rubrifolia* meant that if the name *R. glauca* were to be left in abeyance it would be necessary to take up the next legitimate name in order of priority, which would appear to be *R. rubicuna*.' I am quoting from and indebted to Bean's *Shrubs and Trees Hardy in the British Isles* for the above information, though perhaps indebted is not quite the right word. For the moment, at least, *R. glauca* seems settled on.

This is a species or wild rose native to the more mountainous districts of central and southern Europe. Of tall, arching growth, it is a most distinctive and attractive addition to any garden, but not, as is usual with a rose, because of its flowers. These come in small clusters in early summer, small, pink and very fleeting, though they are followed in the late summer and autumn by round, brilliant red hips, which give every appearance of being in larger clusters than the flowers they came from.

The bright red hips of R. glauca *show up well against the blue-green foliage.*

The hips, however, do not appear until late in the year. Early on it is the almost violet-coloured and practically thornless young shoots that catch the eye, turning to a reddish-brown as they age, and acquiring a few thorns on the way as well. These bear leaves of a greyish-green with a hint of purple, an especially rich colouring when in semi-shade. It takes on a more coppery tone in bright sunlight, and it is for this unique colouring of the shoots and leaves that R. *glauca* is principally grown, not only because they look beautiful and distinctive in the garden but because flower arrangers would find it quite impossible to live without them. In the poor soil of my garden R. *glauca* thrives, growing vigorously and setting seed freely, so that it grows surrounded by small, self-sown seedlings, which friends welcome. This is difficult to reconcile with Jack Harkness's comment, in *Roses*, that it is one of the most obstinate roses to germinate. Contradictory, too, are the comments of both Jack and Graham Thomas, where the latter says: 'In some soils where for any reason R. *rubrifolia* might not thrive – possibly those that are light and sandy – 'Carmenetta' should be tried', while Jack contributes: 'The growth is not always full of vigour, and I think the reason may often be that it does not like to be in wet ground.' Of course, everybody's experience will be different, but from my own observations I tend to go along with the theory that R. *glauca* favours dry ground.

The rose 'Carmenetta' referred to by Graham Thomas is R. *glauca* × R. *rugosa*, raised in Canada in 1930 and not unlike its seed parent, though with the thorns of a rugosa.

R. *glauca* is a wonderful rose to grow as a specimen shrub on its own, perhaps in a bed on the lawn or as a focal point at the end of a path. This is because it is attractive for so many months and not just when it is in flower. In spring come the young shoots, then the flowers, then the older shoots and leaves and finally the display of hips. It will also take its place with credit in a mixed shrub planting, giving an attractive yet blending contrast to the prevailing green of most other kinds.

The small pink blooms of R. glauca *are pleasing but rather fleeting.*

GLOIRE DE DIJON

'I lose no time in stating that the best Climbing Rose with which I am acquainted is Gloire de Dijon, commonly classed with the Tea-scented China roses, but more closely resembling the Noisette family in its robust growth and hardy constitution. Planted against a wall having a southern or eastern aspect, it grows, when once fairly established, with a wonderful luxuriance. I have just measured a lateral on one of my trees, and of the last year's growth, and found it to be 19 feet in length, and the bole of another tree at the base to be nearly 10 inches in circumference. The latter grows on the chancel-wall of my church, and has had two hundred flowers on it in full and simultaneous bloom; nor will the reader desire to arraign me for supersititious practices before a judicial committee when he hears that to this rose I make daily obeisance, because – I only duck to preserve my eyesight. The two trees referred to are on their own roots, but the Rose thrives stoutly on the Brier and the Manetti, budded and grafted, wherever roses grow. Its flowers are the earliest and the latest; it has symmetry, size, endurance, colour (five tints are given to it in the rose catalogues, buff, yellow, orange, fawn, salmon, and it has them all), and perfume. It is what the cricketers call an "all-rounder", good in every point for wall, arcade, pillar, standard, dwarf, *en masse*, or as a single tree. It is easy to cultivate, out of doors and in. It forces admirably, and you may have it, almost in its summer beauty, when Christmas snows are on the ground. With half-a-dozen pots of it, carefully treated, and half-a-dozen trees in your garden, you may enjoy it all year round; and if ever, for some heinous crime, I were miserably sentenced, for the rest of my life, to possess but a single rose tree, I should desire to be supplied, on leaving the dock, with a strong plant of Gloire de Dijon.'

The quotation marks round the above – if not the style – will have indicated that this description is not mine. The more perceptive among those that know me, on noticing the reference to 'the chancel-wall of my church', will have concluded that the piece is, in fact, an extract from *A Book About Roses* by S. Reynolds Hole, later to become Dean of Rochester and co-founder and first President of the National Rose Society in 1876.

This means that what he had to say about 'Gloire de Dijon' was written nearly 120 years ago, so that it is natural to wonder how the rose has stood the test of time. Pretty well, on the whole, although it is only the exceptional plant nowadays that has quite the vigour he describes. It is said that there is now a good strain and a poor strain of 'Gloire de Dijon', which may be true, but it is one of those statements that is very hard to pin down. For a would-be buyer it is not very helpful either, for how could one tell if such a rose is good or bad until it is really established, by which time it is rather late in the day to find out. That authority on climbing roses from across the Atlantic, G.A. Stevens, writing in 1933, had this to say, of 'Gloire de Dijon' in America: 'For some reason, the gigantic plants formerly so very common are seldom seen nowadays; some observers fear a deterioration of the variety has set in.' So perhaps the answer is not that there is a good and a bad strain but that there is a general lessening in vigour.

Despite all this, it is still a very worthwhile rose to have and retains most of the qualities detailed so vividly by Dean Hole. It was raised in France by Jacotot in 1853 and the parentage is thought to have been an unknown tea rose × 'Souvenir de la Malmaison', which is a bourbon. Thus it is properly called a climbing tea rose, but because it is so much hardier than all others in that group, many authorities place it among the noisettes. I would not quarrel with that, though at one time, around the turn of the century, 'Gloire de Dijon' was placed in a group under the collective name of Dijon teas, M. Jacotot having been a native of that town. Other climbing teas also in that category were 'Billard et Barre',

'Bouquet d'Or' and 'Mme Bérard'. 'Bouquet d'Or' had 'Gloire de Dijon' as a pollen parent and 'Mme Bérard' had it as a seed parent. Other than the fact that they were both climbing tea roses, I can find no direct link between 'Gloire de Dijon' and 'Billard et Barre'. The latter was not even raised in Dijon but came from Pernet-Ducher of Lyon.

'Gloire de Dijon' is too strong-growing for a pillar, but is fine for a wall, arch (of reasonable size) or pergola. On a wall the only minus mark might be given for a tendency to bareness low down, but that is a fault that it shares with a very considerable number of other climbers. It is still freely available, and not just from specialist growers.

'Gloire de Dijon' dates from the last century but is still unbeatable in its colour range.

GOLDEN SHOWERS

This is one of the most popular of modern climbers and an especially useful one, too, in that it fills a gap. In training a climbing rose one is always advised to fan the shoots out sideways, tying them in to horizontal wires to encourage flowering side shoots to break into growth. However, it is frustrating to be told this if you live in a house, perhaps in the Georgian style, in which the windows are tall and quite close together. There will be no room to spread the shoots of a climber sideways and the same may apply with a small, modern bungalow or an old cottage.

'Golden Showers' is an excellent pillar rose.

This is where 'Golden Showers' is so useful, for it is naturally an upright grower and is one of the few roses that will flower well low down as well as at the top, even without any special training. Quite how it does this is difficult to say, for a chemical growth inhibitor is supposed to prevent flowering shoots from breaking from the buds low down if the main shoots are allowed to grow straight up. Only when the main shoots are fanned out does this inhibitor cease to function, so clearly there is something special about 'Golden Showers'. It is certainly the most suitable rose to fill tall, narrow spaces, growing to a height of about 8–10ft (2.4–3m).

Some say that it could have a better coverage of leaves and it is difficult to argue with this, but those that are there are a rich, deep green, glossy and generally free from disease. The blooms come on long, practically thornless stems, the pointed buds opening to rather loosely formed, bright yellow flowers some 4–5in (10–12cm) across and with dark stamens at the heart. They fade quite quickly to a paler yellow and then almost to white, but maintain their attractiveness throughout. Rather surprisingly, they hold their colour longer and last extremely well when used as cut flowers, for which their long stems make them particularly suitable.

Fairly large hips form if the rose is not dead-headed, but it is not a tall enough climber to make cutting them off difficult. Then you will be rewarded with some flowers throughout the summer and a very good second flush in early autumn. The scent is sweet, though, it must be said, not particularly strong.

Good yellow recurrent climbers are not numerous. We are lucky to have 'Golden Showers'.

'Golden Showers' was bred in America and, unlike many of its fellows, has crossed the Atlantic in fine form. It was raised by Dr W.E. Lammerts from his own hybrid tea 'Charlotte Armstrong' crossed with the creamy-yellow climbing hybrid tea 'Captain Thomas'. There is the blood of the golden-yellow hybrid perpetual 'Soeur Thérèse' one generation back which probably contributed to 'Golden Showers' fine, strong colour. It was introduced by Germain of Los Angeles in 1956, and rapidly gained a tremendous reputation world-wide as a thoroughly reliable rose, which was, as one writer put it, 'all gloss and smartness'.

The uses of 'Golden Showers' are not, of course, confined to tall, narrow walls. It will grow on any wall, even a north-facing one (it is one of the best of roses for this) and is ideal, too, for training on a pillar. Its fairly stiff upright habit does not really make it the best rose for an arch or pergola, though it can be used attractively to clothe the upright pillars of the latter, even if it will not drape itself over the top. That can be left to the ramblers.

If pruned suitably hard, 'Golden Showers' will make an attractive free-standing shrub and I have also used it, planted about 2–3ft (60–90cm) apart, as a flowering hedge. It can get along quite well like this as it needs no further support other than that provided by the branches of its neighbours interlocking, one with another.

'Golden Showers' is not the only rose that can be used in the kind of awkward spaces described earlier. If you favour a sparkling white, then 'White Cockade' is the rose for you; if you want a fairly dazzling red flushed yellow (or yellow flushed red, according to how you look at it), try 'Joseph's Coat'. Neither of these will outgrow their allotted space but you can, if you wish, and favour something in pink, try one of the bourbon roses such as 'Mme Ernst Calvat', which, as a family, will climb quite well against a wall, although not usually grown in this way.

GOLDEN WINGS

A number of good, medium-sized, single-flowered, repeat-flowering shrub roses such as 'Rosy Cushion' and 'Smarty' have been introduced in recent years, both of them, and others not unlike them, catalogued as 'ground cover' varieties. The reasons for this may be clear to those responsible for marketing them but are a mystery to the rest of us, to whom they are straightforward, reasonably spreading shrubs growing up to about 4–5 ft (1.2–1.5 m).

Nobody, as far as I am aware, has ever claimed that another rose, to which the same general description applies, could be used for ground cover, though that may be because ground cover plants were not the latest fashion when it was introduced in 1953. The rose in question is 'Golden Wings', that most lovely of single varieties, which bears, non-stop, tremendous numbers of 4in (10cm), pale yellow, single blooms. It is bushy and branches freely, reaching a height of 5ft (1.5m) and sometimes a little more. Ideal for specimen planting, it will also mix well with other shrubs in a sunny border, providing late flowers with its second main flush of blooms. The plentiful leaves are of hybrid-tea type, semi-glossy and very resistant to disease, although I have seen black spot late on in a bad season.

Wanting to know what the breeding line of such a good rose could be, I went to Roy Shepherd's book, *History of the Rose*, for he was the man who raised 'Golden Wings'. He gives it as 'a seedling of *R. spinosissima (R. pimpinellifolia)* × 'Soeur Thérèse' and, rather surprised that this first-generation cross between a species and a hybrid tea should have produced a recurrent-flowering variety, I delved a

A single bloom of 'Golden Wings' is a thing of great beauty and it is fragrant, too.

little further. Jack Harkness's encyclopaedic *Roses*, to which I have already referred several times and which is ninety-nine times out of a hundred dependable, gives the following: 'Soeur Thérèse' × (*R. spinosissima altaica* × 'Ormiston Roy'), the last a hybrid of two species and non-recurrent. This same parentage is given in The Royal National Rose Society's publication *Roses to Enjoy* and could be right as Roy Shepherd's reference to a *spinosissima* seedling is not very precise. At any rate, there is certainly a strong Scotch rose influence, but precious little indication of it in the finished result. There are none of the wickedly prickly stems so typical of Scotch roses and very large blooms with a scent quite foreign to the pimpinellifolias.

Roy Shepherd has for far too long been confined to the annex of the house of fame. His *History of the Rose* was first published in 1954 and, though one of the best books on roses written in recent times, never made the sort of impact that was its due. It went out of print and vanished from the scene, perhaps handicapped by its title, which indicates a much more limited scope than that actually covered. It was not until a small and dedicated group within the American Heritage Roses organization did something about it that the book was brought back, in a facsimile edition, in 1978, and what a wealth of information it revealed to those who had not seen it before. That distinguished American rosarian, Lily Schohan, first suggested the reissue of the book and perhaps I might quote briefly from the introduction to it, in which she wrote:

'One of the outstanding values of Mr Shepherd's work is that he did not just list species and horticultural clones; he also provided all known synonyms. He states of *R. cinamonea plena* for instance that it was also known as *R. foecundissima*, *R. gorenkensis*, *R. majalis*, Rose du Mai, Rose de Pâques, Rose du Saint Sacrement and Whitsuntide Rose. An old name for a rose can thus be looked up in the index and referred back to the modern name for that plant. Moreover, the index is divided into a general index and an index of rose names; the latter lists names not mentioned in the text with the synonyms under which they may be found given in parentheses.'

Shepherd grew some 3500 roses in his own garden and his writings excelled in reducing an exceedingly complex jumble of plants to an orderly arrangement in a style both clear and non-technical. He was awarded the American Gold Honor Medal in 1954 for 'distinguished service to old roses and their history'.

He and his wife Ann had a happy knack when it came to choosing the names of the roses they introduced to commerce. In addition to 'Golden Wings' there were 'Flirtation', 'Courtship', 'June Bride', 'Wedding Ring' and 'Lullaby'; but 'Golden Wings' is the only one to remain in the nursery lists and is a more than fitting memorial to a man whose death in 1962 was a real loss to the rose world and to the delvers into the forgotten byways of rose history.

'Golden Wings' will make a colourful hedge or a free-standing shrub on its own.

GRAHAM THOMAS

In describing 'Constance Spry' I covered the very early experiments by nurseryman David Austin in his attempts to breed a recurrent habit and modern colours into roses that resembled the old garden roses in form. In 'Constance Spry' he created a wonderful rose, very similar to those from the past (and rather better in many ways than a number of the genuine old ones) but it was not recurrent, the achieving of which was a primary aim. Another fine rose, which he called 'Chianti', appeared in 1967. In its crimson petals this captured the old rose fragrance, was more restrained in growth than 'Constance Spry', but again was once flowering. The Le Grice floribunda 'Dusky Maiden' and the deep crimson gallica 'Tuscany' were the parents.

Recurrence did, however, come in time when other roses both old and new were crossed with 'Constance Spry'. Varieties that were introduced into the breeding line included 'Aloha' (which was to prove very influential), the pink floribunda 'Ma Perkins' from America and, going back a bit to 1890, the early hybrid tea 'Mme Caroline Testout'. 'Iceberg' was another rose that has passed on many of its good qualities over the years.

During the 1960s and 1970s 'Chianti' was not the only good rose produced, but it must be said that David's quest for perfection was not all smooth going. As he now admits, it was probably the excitement and enthusiasm generated by his pioneering work that induced him to put on the market a number of varieties that had better have been kept in the nursery fields. They included a series named for characters in Chaucer's *Canterbury Tales* and included 'The Squire' (deep crimson), 'The Prioress' (blush-white), 'The Nun' (white), 'The Miller' (pink) and, by far the best of the lot, 'Wife of Bath'. The last made a sturdy little bush about 3ft (1m) tall with clear pink blooms which paled toward the petal edges and which opened cupped and repeated well. With all this group recurrence had been achieved but, with the honourable exception of 'Wife of Bath', they had beautiful flowers but poor, spindly growth. With such thin stems to support them, the flowers hung their heads and much of their charm was lost.

The deep, golden yellow of 'Graham Thomas' and its fine fragrance make it a winner.

A bed of 'Graham Thomas' looks spectacular, but it is a big rose, needing space.

Other varieties were introduced, showing steady progress towards the ideal, and there were some very good roses among them. Then, at the beginning of the 1980s, there appeared to be a sudden step forward. 'Abraham Darby', for instance, arrived, which in this case had two comparatively modern roses as its parents, 'Yellow Cushion' and 'Aloha'. It bears its fragrant double blooms with their blend of yellow, pink and apricot, on a strong-growing, arching shrub that will grow to about 5ft (1.5m) or can be used as a short climber. Others that came along were equally good and it was clear that a time was approaching when David Austin could say that his ultimate goal was in sight. Other nurseries began to stock a selection of his roses, which they would not have done had the demand not been there.

Going back a little, both the splendidly vivid yellow floribunda/shrub 'Chinatown' and 'Golden Wings' had been used in the hybridizing quite early on. Possibly their robust growth and colours influenced the apricot-yellow blooms of 'Charles Austin', another successful variety dating from 1973.

This became one of the parents of 'Graham Thomas', ten years later, the other being 'Iceberg' × a seedling. Certainly one can discern a lot of the qualities of 'Chinatown' in what has proved to be the best and most successful Austin rose to date. The yellow of the blooms of 'Graham Thomas' is, however, of a deeper tone than that of 'Chinatown', and there is a hint of apricot in the early stages. The flowers open cupped and are normally of medium size, though every now and then an exceptionally large one appears. There is a strong tea-rose fragrance. The plant will grow strongly to 4ft (1.2m), though I have seen it on occasion go a good deal above this, and breaks freely from the base with a constant supply of new shoots to flower in their turn. David Austin himself has had reports of 'Graham Thomas' reaching 10ft (3m) in South Africa but one would not expect that in the climate of the UK. The foliage is plentiful and of a bright, shiny green, generally free from the attacks of black spot and mildew. A wonderful rose for a hedge or for a group planting in perhaps threes or fours.

GREAT MAIDEN'S BLUSH

This is the second alba rose in our selection, after our opener, R. × *alba* 'Semi-plena'. In describing the latter, a white rose, it was said that the majority of albas, despite their name, were pink. Here is one of the pink ones, from some time prior to the fifteenth century, which can still be found growing in gardens that also possibly date back that far, both in the UK and on the continent of Europe. It is always reliable and always of great charm, with its delicate blush-pink double flowers, the petals reflexing to a pale creamy-pink at their edges.

An indication of its popularity over the years can be gained from the number of names under which it has been marketed and grown; they include: 'La Royale', 'La Séduisante', 'Cuisse de Nymphe', 'La Virginale', 'Incarnata', R. *carnea*, R. *rubicans*, R. *alba rubincunda* and, of course, 'Great Maiden's Blush', this last the only one of its names that can be attributed to the United Kingdom. To Redouté it was R. *alba regalis*, but otherwise in France it was generally 'Cuisse de Nymphe' or even 'Cuisse de Nymphe Émue' ('Thigh of the Passionate Nymph'), which is such an evocative name that it was a pity it was not adopted universally.

Although it is certainly much older, records seem to start at Kew Gardens in 1797; but it is better, I think, to be non-committal about the age of 'Great Maiden's Blush' and simply to say, perhaps not very originally, that 'age cannot wither nor custom stale its infinite variety'.

Whenever it may have first appeared, its quality must have been evident from the start. It is one of the best of the larger shrub roses, fairly upright and reaching 7ft (2.1m) or so in height and about 5ft (1.5m) across. June, through into July, is the time of flowering, and this will be profuse. Afterwards the usual very attractive grey-green leaves of the alba family take over, to carry it through as an asset to any garden until the autumn. It will be at home in a large shrub border, as a specimen plant perhaps in a round bed on a lawn, or when used as a hedging plant. Situated against a wall it may go considerably over its accustomed height and can be very impressive, but it is really best used as a shrub rather than a climber. For a rose with such double flowers it stands up to rain remarkably well, as do those of 'Maiden's Blush' (also called 'Small Maiden's Blush'), a smaller version which is very similar apart from its size.

Something remarkably like 'Great Maiden's Blush' is depicted in paintings of the Italian Renaissance and it is almost certainly the rose described in John Parkinson's *Paradisi in Sole Paradisus Terrestris* of 1629. Under the name Incarnation Rose, he says of it: '. . . in most things like unto the White Rose, both for the growing of the stock, and the bigness of the flower; but that it is more spaced abroad than the white when it is blown, and is of a pale blush colour all the flower throughout'.

I must confess that it was a toss-up as to whether I gave my vote to 'Great Maiden's Blush' rather than 'Celestial' (aka 'Céleste') when choosing one of the pink albas to describe. The latter is similar in growth and size, but has the most exquisite soft pink, semi-double flowers, each with a crown of golden stamens. Gertrude Jekyll referred to it as 'a rose of wonderful beauty when the bud is half opened'.

Redouté, on the other hand, considered it a damask, and it appears in his collection as *R. damascena* 'Aurora'. A good story, though unconfirmed, is that 'Celeste' is the Minden Rose, which commemorates the successful action of British troops at the Battle of Minden against the much larger French army under Ferdinand of Brunswick in 1759, during the Seven Years' War. Passing through an orchard while following up the fleeing French, the soldiers each plucked a rose to wear as a battle honour. Since the date was 1 August, one must speculate as to which rose it could have been, since all roses with the exception of the autumn damask would at that period have long since finished flowering. Certainly 'Celeste' would not have been blooming, but whatever the rose, to this day the battalions of the Suffolk Regiment wear roses in their head-dress. They are, however, red and yellow roses, these being the regimental colours.

Brief mention should be made of two other fine alba roses. 'Queen of Denmark' (I use the English translation of the name since no one seems to agree how the original Danish name should be spelled) is not a typical alba, being of more slender, branching growth with leaves of a much darker green than one would expect. The flowers are enchanting, very double and of a deeper pink than the other albas, with a touch of carmine at the centre. Often they are quartered. With the second variety, 'Félicité Parmentier', we are back once more to the palest blush-pink, though the rounded buds have a distinct pale primrose tint before they open. This variety is a much shorter grower than the others and so is suitable for a small garden.

When planting, bear in mind that, if on their own roots, albas can sucker and eventually become a nuisance. However, they are not such a menace in this respect as the gallicas or the pimpinellifolias.

'Great Maiden's Blush' has been a favourite since at least early in the 18th century.

ICEBERG

Although all rose breeders must be both optimists and dreamers, one cannot help wondering whether the German hybridist Reimer Kordes realized, when he first crossed the rather undistinguished shrubby polyantha-type rose 'Robin Hood' with the shapely but distinctly frail hybrid tea 'Virgo', just what he was creating. It turned out, of course, to be 'Iceberg', possibly the most famous floribunda ever produced, though it can be said that a very different result might well have been on the cards.

What, for instance, might have happened if, when introducing it in 1958, Herr Kordes had put it on the market as a hybrid musk rather than a floribunda? He could have done so, for one of 'Iceberg's parents, as we have seen, was 'Robin Hood'. This, though very much a polyantha in appearance and ancestry, was sold as a hybrid musk when it came on the scene in 1927. It was one of Joseph Pemberton's famous collection, although by the time 'Robin Hood' appeared in the Pemberton nursery list, its creator had died. However, with this rose on one side of the equation and a hybrid tea on the other, the breeding of 'Iceberg' would appear to make it just as much a hybrid musk as Pemberton's 'Moonlight' or 'Prosperity'. One suspects that, if it had been classed with them it would have languished for many years in the back pages of nursery lists as did the Pemberton varieties, until the comparatively recent increase in interest in shrub rose gardening.

Yet, introduced as a floribunda, albeit in a colour not usually associated in the rose trade with bestsellerdom, 'Iceberg' still features in the vast majority

'Iceberg's flowers have a sweet fragrance.

OPPOSITE: *If only lightly pruned, 'Iceberg' will make a 5ft (1.5m) shrub, almost always in flower.*

of nursery catalogues and, after all this time, still tops the list of the best and most popular floribundas compiled each year from votes by members of the Royal National Rose Society. It was selected as well to the World Federation of Rose Societies' Hall of Fame, only being preceded by 'Peace' and 'Queen Elizabeth', and over the years it has never really had a rival. A very good McGredy floribunda called 'Icewhite' tried for a while, but could not stand up to the competition and faded away. 'Ivory Fashion' was perhaps more successful, at least in America, but never really established itself in the United

Kingdom. More recently, 'Margaret Merril' has come on the scene as a contender for 'Iceberg's crown with the advantage of a notably strong, sweet fragrance. It has, however, a marked tendency to black spot and, attractive as it is, I do not feel it will prevail. It is a more conventional floribunda in its growth, carrying its flowers only in large trusses on the top of long, strong, straight shoots, whereas 'Iceberg', with its freely branching growth, is attractive both in its flowers and as a shrub.

In fact, although it will make an impressive bedding rose, 'Iceberg' is best grown as a shrub or else as a standard. There can be a tendency sometimes to black spot, which is much less evident if the bushes are not crowded together, and light pruning, so that the rose is free to grow 4–5ft (1.2–1.5m) tall, will result in a better leaf colour. In bedding, the leaves tend to take on a more yellowish green, which does not form such an attractive background for the flowers and, as they grow right down the sides of the bush, many of them will be hidden by close planting.

As a standard, 'Iceberg' will make a very large and quite spectacular head, as can be seen in many a garden while driving through the country in the summer. A strong stake is essential to cope with the weight and wind resistance of such prolific growth – the head will probably reach 4ft (1.2m) across.

The fairly large and moderately full blooms of 'Iceberg', which open from attractively scrolled buds, are white with an occasional pink tinge, especially after they have been open for a while. Slightly scented, they are carried in great profusion and good continuity in both large and small trusses, the blooms lasting well when cut. This quality makes 'Iceberg' a favourite rose for exhibitors of floribundas. It is also a favourite with flower arrangers for there is a certain daintiness and grace about the way the blooms are carried on the stems. Weather resistance is above average, but prolonged rain can cause some pink spotting on the flowers.

A Royal National Rose Society Gold Medal winner in 1958 and of numerous other overseas awards, 'Iceberg' is known as 'Fée des Neiges' in France and as 'Schneewittchen' in its country of origin. The translation of the latter is Snow Witch, which is really a much more suitable name for any rose, let alone one as elegant as 'Iceberg'.

And so to one final note about a remarkable rose. In 1968 in England, 'Iceberg' produced a climbing sport which has turned out to be one of the best white, repeat-flowering climbers, vigorous and prolific in bloom. Could any raiser's dream possibly have seen a future such as this as he brushed the pollen of one rose on to the stigmas of another?

As a bedding rose 'Iceberg' is unbeatable, with fine, light green leaves and branching growth.

JUST JOEY

F ew people would disagree, I think, with the fact that too many new roses are introduced each year, a number almost indistinguishable from those that have gone before, and how many of them survive? One has only to think of the features in gardening magazines each year on the new roses at Chelsea. Stars of stage and screen will be seen beaming from the pages behind a large bouquet of a new rose that has been named after them in the hope that it will get something of an additional boost. Presumably the celebrity after whom a rose is named will grow the dozen bushes of it with which he or she has been presented, but does anyone else? With the honourable exception of a few like 'Anna Ford' and 'Hannah Gordon', such roses have, as a rule, a very brief moment of glory.

Some other roses may have gone through the trials conducted by the Royal National Rose Society at the Gardens of the Rose near St Albans, or through trials conducted by the rose trade, but the proportion of winners is very small and even some of these roses, too, may fall by the wayside.

Rather a depressing picture on the whole, making one wonder how rose hybridists retain their enthusiasm. It is the enthusiasm, of course, of a gambler, and gambles do pay off now and then, so that a winning rose may appear from amongst the apparent also-rans. Such a one was 'Just Joey'.

It did not have a particularly impressive start and gained only a Trial Ground Certificate in the RNRS trials in the early 1970s. In those days new seedling varieties still in the trials and not yet available on the market would be shown at the Rose Festival at St

The remarkable flower form of 'Just Joey' is well shown here.

Albans and the public asked to judge them. In the summer show of 1971 'Just Joey' swept the board, no doubt largely due to its wonderful pale coppery-orange colouring and unique flower form with its waved petals that scorn triumphantly the usual high centre of the modern hybrid tea. The blooms are some 5in (12cm) or more across. A mixture of 'Fragrant Cloud' as the pollen parent and the golden-yellow 'Dr Verhage' as the seed parent had produced a wonderful rose, lacking only the former's fine fragrance.

The coppery pink of 'Just Joey' becomes paler with time.

The flowers appear, always one to a stem, on a bush that grows to an average height of, say, 30in (75cm), with fine, dark green, semi-glossy foliage, though there could with advantage be a few more leaves on the upper stems. Despite this, it makes the almost perfect bedding rose and is also good as a cut flower.

Introduced in 1973, the public, now able to buy it, took this rose to its heart and in 1986 it gained the James Mason Memorial Gold Medal which is given each year to 'the rose which has given most pleasure over the past fifteen years'. On top of this, in 1994 it came top in the voting for the World's Favourite Rose', a poll organized by the World Federation of Rose Societies, which gave a clear indication that 'Just Joey's popularity had spread world-wide.

'Just Joey' was raised by Roger Pawsey of the old-established rose nursery Cants of Colchester. Originally it was intended to call the rose 'Joey Pawsey' after Roger's wife Joey. Somehow this sounded a bit of a tongue-twister and Roger's father remarked, 'Why not call it just 'Joey'? Whether from a mishearing of the suggestion or perhaps from pure inspiration, it was decided to use both words and 'Just Joey' the rose became. Roger has been President of the British Association of Rose Breeders and has other hybridizing successes to his name. He was responsible for, among others, 'Goldstar', which won a Gold Medal at The Hague, 'Alpine Sunset' and 'English Miss'. A rose-growing family to the core, Roger's sister Angela originated and edits that brilliant yearly publication *Find That Rose*.

KORRESIA

Except that breeding in the rose world never stands still, one could say that 'Korresia' is the culmination of some eighty or so years' work by hybridists world-wide, attempting to produce a bright yellow, healthy, scented, unfading floribunda with a good constitution.

Until the very beginning of this century, apart from species or near species roses such as *R. ecae*, *R. foetida* and *R. harisonii* ('Harison's Yellow'), there were no bright yellow roses in our gardens. The predominant colours of the roses grown until that time had been mauve, a purplish red, maroon, lilac, white, and a wide range of pinks, with crimson to be found in some of the China roses. Orange and flame colours, as well as yellow, were absent.

This was clearly a situation which no self-respecting rose breeder could ignore, but it took many years of patient work before the first success, by Joseph Pernet-Ducher of Lyon. To introduce yellow into his breeding lines he used a wild rose from the Middle East, *R. foetida* 'Persiana' (the 'Persian Yellow'), a double-flowered form of *R. foetida*, crossing it with a number of hybrid perpetual varieties, which were the fashionable garden roses of that time. In 1900, he put on the market 'Soleil d'Or', which was very much a hybrid perpetual in appearance, with double, fragrant blooms in a mixture of yellow and orange-red. Still available from specialist nurseries, it is obviously not a true yellow. It was, however, introduced as such and was undoubtedly a tremendous step forward – it led directly to the introduction in 1910 of one of its offspring, 'Rayon d'Or', which was true golden yellow.

No one else came near to matching Pernet-Ducher's achievements (as a result of them he became known as the Wizard of Lyon), so that the results of his work can be said to be found in all our modern yellow garden roses. All have the blood of *R. foetida* in them, even if by now very much diluted by the mixing in of other strains. Just the same, the use of this rose, although it introduced a completely new colour range (for orange and flame colours must be attributed to it as well), also brought a number of less desirable traits. *R. foetida*, and through it the 'Persian Yellow', proved in the climate of the West to be a martyr to black spot which, although known to exist, not been a particular problem for European gardeners. The Persian rose passed on this particular weakness to all its progeny and, as the early Pernet-Ducher roses were crossed by other breeders with practically every rose they could find, in the hope of a winner to match the success of 'Rayon d'Or', black spot was spread far and wide and is now to be found in roses of every hue.

Again, whereas *R. foetida* has a rather unusual smell of its own and 'Soleil d'Or' was scented, in general the yellow roses that followed it were noticeably lacking in fragrance. Moreover, their constitution left much to be desired. One might think that a rose coming from a hotter climate would not thrive in the dampness and frosts of a European winter, but in fact *R. foetida* does rather well in the United Kingdom. For some reason, however, many of its descendants have tended to be not very robust and to suffer from die-back. And finally, in the catalogue of minus factors deriving from *R. foetida*, although it

*'Korresia' won no awards but came to the fore through its
quality as a yellow bedding rose.*

'Arthur Bell' was probably the next noteworthy
yellow floribunda, a full ten years after the introduction of 'Allgold'. It was a first-class rose in all ways
except for its lack of colour-fastness. One of its
parents was 'Cläre Grammerstorf', which also
appears in the pedigree of 'Korresia', although the
latter's immediate forbears were the yellow floribunda 'Friedrich Worlein' from Kordes and the
American-raised 'Spanish Sun', from which, perhaps, it inherited its strong fragrance.

'Korresia' (also known as 'Friesia' and 'Sun-
sprite'), came on the scene in 1974, produced by the
German nursery of W. Kordes Sohne. It was argua-
bly slower in making its mark in the United
Kingdom than it might have been had it gone
through the trials at the Royal National Rose
Society's Gardens of the Rose, where it would
almost certainly have won one of the top awards.
Nobody appears to be quite sure what happened, but
it does seem that, although 'Korresia' was entered
for the trials, somehow a wrong (and obviously less
good) variety was sent. It was some time before the
mistake was discovered, too late to rectify it. The
trials last for three years and 'Korresia' was more
than ready before they were over. It came on the
market without the benefit of the boost an award can
give, but did not take too long to reach the top
through sheer merit.

It is now considered one of the best of all bedding roses, not too tall at an average height of 2½ft
(75cm), with large, bright green leaves that set off
the golden-yellow, unfading blooms to perfection.
The double flowers have a sweet scent and open flat
from shapely buds. They are carried in medium-sized
trusses with a good repeat after the first flush in late
June. The plant's upright, sturdy growth is ideal for
bedding purposes, when it should be planted about
2½ft (75cm) apart. Even with close planting, disease
is rarely a problem, though the Rose Society's show
bed did get infected by a virus which affected the
foliage. This, however, appears to have been an
isolated incident and has not been reported elsewhere. Certainly not from my own garden.

retains its own bright colour well, the yellow roses
that have followed have, until comparatively recent
years, tended to fade quite quickly to a cream shade
in strong sunlight.

So those who took up the challenge of producing the perfect yellow garden rose had a lot of
problems to overcome before a variety like 'Korresia' could be created. Breeding a new rose is a slow
process, with the transition from a seed to a market-
able variety taking, as was said earlier, anything up to
eight years to achieve. Since the introduction of
'Rayon d'Or' a multitude of yellow roses has been
produced with greater or lesser claims to perfection
from their breeders but, until the coming of the
floribunda 'Allgold' from the Norfolk breeder
Edward Le Grice in 1956, no rose had really overcome all the drawbacks that the use of *R. foetida* had
brought. True, 'Allgold' was only very slightly
scented, but it was a good, healthy rose of robust
growth and the bright yellow of its flowers was quite
unfading. It was continuously in bloom throughout
the summer and came from a cross between the once
very popular pale yellow 'Goldilocks' and the deep
yellow hybrid tea 'Ellinor Le Grice'. It is still widely
stocked, though perhaps it is beginning to go down-
hill a little, as most roses do after a number of years.

OPPOSITE: *Many early yellow roses faded badly in hot
sunlight; 'Korresia' holds it colour well.*

MADAME ALFRED CARRIÈRE

Raised in 1879 by J. Schwartz of Lyon in France, 'Mme Alfred Carrière' is one of a pair of climbing roses that seem usually to be linked together in people's minds, the other being the very different 'Mme Grégoire Staechelin'. The latter has not been going for anything like the same length of time, having been put on the market in 1927, but both have the distinction of being in virtually every grower's catalogue since they were introduced and of still appearing side by side in the RNRS Rose Analysis, 'Mme Grégoire Staechelin' in sixteenth place and 'Mme Alfred Carrière' in seventeenth. A bigger achievement for the older rose of the two, of course, but not many roses can match the track record of either of them. Only one other popular climber, 'Zéphirine Drouhin', of 1873, can beat it.

'Mme Alfred Carrière' is a prodigious grower that can very rapidly cover the wall of a good-sized house and then start sending long, strong canes out into space looking for new territory to conquer. For some reason it is usually described as stiff in growth, but it has been anything but that in my experience, being flexible and easy to train, if not to contain. The flowers are creamy white with a faint pink flush, opening from firm round buds, cupped but rather loosely formed and with many petals. They are extremely fragrant and those who have seen it on one of the walls at Mottisfont Abbey garden or on the wall of the cottage at Sissinghurst Castle will not need to be told what a magnificent display it will put on each year in early summer. Seldom without some flowers thereafter, it will have a second later flush, although hardly as dramatic as the first. The long,

rather thin shoots are smooth and have very few thorns. The foliage is bright green and plentiful, though it should be noted that new growth can be attacked by mildew in the autumn.

The pedigree of 'Mme Alfred Carrière' is not known, but it is generally thought to belong to the noisette group, even though to the layman there are few noisette characteristics and the scent is more like that of a modern rose.

The noisettes originated in America in Charleston, South Carolina, with a rice farmer named John Champneys. He appears to have grown the genuine musk rose in his garden and also the China rose 'Old Blush'; and whether by deliberate hybridization or by chance, the two were joined and the issue was to be named 'Champneys' Pink Cluster'. Philippe Noisette, a French nurseryman living in Charleston, obtained and sowed seeds of this and the first noisette rose was the result. This was 'Blush Noisette', which Philippe sent in 1817 to his brother Louis, also a nurseryman but in Paris, where Redouté was to paint it. From it other hybrids were obtained. Thereafter Joseph Pemberton, writing at the turn of the century, takes up the story: 'They were hardy and vigorous, but most of them have gone out of cultivation. One, however, remains, the pure white, almost evergreen rose, 'Aimée Vibert', sent out by Vibert in 1828. Later on, through crossing with varieties of the Tea-scented Rose, the Noisette approached more

OPPOSITE: *'Mme Alfred Carrière' flowers non-stop all summer and is extremely fragrant.*

'Mme Alfred Carrière' will soon cover the wall of a house, even if it faces to the north.

nearly to the Tea, although it retained its special features in perfume and growth; 'Lamarque' (1830), 'Ophirie' (1841) and 'Céline Forestier' being good examples of this period.'

This is, of course, where 'Mme Alfred Carrière, if indeed it is a noisette, fits in, among the late tea crosses, but Pemberton was wrong in suggesting that so few noisettes remain. Others still grown, whilst mostly obtainable only through specialist growers, include 'Alister Stella Gray', 'Bouquet d'Or', 'Chromatella', 'Claire Jacquier', 'Desprez à Fleur Jaune', 'L'Idéal', 'Manetti', 'Maréchal Niel', 'Rêve d'Or', 'William Allen Richardson' and, the queen of them all, 'Gloire de Dijon'.

MADAME HARDY

All descriptions of 'Mme Hardy' tell us that it was introduced in 1832 by Eugène Hardy, who had raised it in the Luxembourg Gardens in Paris (of which he was director) and named it after his wife. That is all, but M. Hardy was not just a one-rose man and deserves to have a little more said about him. It was under his authority that experiments were carried out with the breeding of *Hulthema persica*, with its small, yellow, red-eyed flowers, resulting in × *Hulthema hardii*, at one time within the genus *Rosa*, which led many years later to the highly original breeding programme by Jack Harkness and Alex

'Mme Hardy', showing its distinctive green 'eye'.

Cocker already referred to on page 40. This Middle-Eastern plant, as was mentioned earlier, is depicted as *Rosa berberifolia* in Redouté's *Les Roses*, and it seems to have been a case of one minute it is a rose, the next moment it is not. The relationship would probably have been clear to M. Hardy, who was also the man who imported 'Parks's Yellow Tea-Scented China' into France in 1824 for the Royal Luxembourg Gardens, after Parks had brought it from China for the RHS the previous year. The latter was one of the roses that became known as the stud Chinas, meaning that its descendants, together with those of 'Hume's Blush Tea-Scented China', 'Parson's Pink China' ('Old Blush') and 'Slater's Crimson China', were to have such a dramatic influence on the development of the roses in our gardens. It was they that led directly to a radical change in flower form and the coming of the high-centred hybrid tea.

'Mme Hardy' comes from a very ancient family, the damasks, generally thought to have arrived in the West from the environs of Damascus. William Robinson is on record as stating that they were 'brought to Europe about 1270 by Thibault IV, Count of Brie, returning from a crusade in the Holy Land'. Where he obtained such precise information I do not know, or whether or not it is true, but in Roman times they were well established in Italy. From the descriptions of Roman writers such as Pliny the Elder there can be little doubt that at least some of the roses then grown, largely for their magical perfumes and the oils that were extracted from them, were damasks. This family of roses has also been used for some hundreds of years in Turkey

and the mountain valleys of Bulgaria and the Balkans generally for the distillation of attar of roses. Scent is a notable characteristic of the family.

Nobody knows for certain the parentage of 'Mme Hardy' although there is some doubt that it is of pure damask lineage. Almost certainly a centifolia is in there somewhere and one could, I suppose, say that the blooms are more gallica in their formation than damask. However, for its description I cannot do better than repeat more or less what I said in my book *Shrub Roses, Climbers and Ramblers*: 'Many people think that it has the most beautiful blooms of all the old roses. They open from buds with long, feathery calyces and are sometimes blush-tinted at first. Fully expanded they are of the purest white, flat and quartered, with a green carpel in the centre. This is not a feature confined to 'Mme Hardy', but against the whiteness of the surrounding petals of this particular rose it is extremely distinctive. The flowers come on side shoots which are often long and may be weighed down by the size of the clusters. The blooms are not fond of rain but otherwise last over a long period. The bush grows to some 4–5ft and is generally reckoned to spread out to about the same distance. I have seen it do this in several gardens, but in mine it stays much more upright and compact. There are matt, light green leaves which are not completely proof against mildew. Sweet scent.' I might now add that the leaves are a magnet to the leaf-rolling sawfly, but the position in which my 'Mme Hardy' grows is rather hemmed in by trees and the air is still, which appears to encourage these pests. The rather soft green leaves of 'Mme Hardy' could not be in greater contrast to the tough, glossy, leathery texture of those of 'Peace' – or, indeed, to those of 'Chinatown' – yet both these varieties are just as subject to attack from the sawflies. Applying a caterpillar spray in late April and again a couple of times in May may help a little and, if the attack is not too bad, the affected leaves can be picked off.

All in all, however, 'Mme Hardy' is a general favourite. William Paul, writing in 1848, said that this one variety would suffice to make M. Hardy's name famous but there was one dissenting voice, at least in part. It was a favourite with Dean Hole, but he added to his praise the following: '... but alas!

"Green-eyed" like "Jealousy" – envious it may be of Madame Zoutman, who, though not of such clear complexion, is free from ocular infirmities'. 'Mme Zoutman', or 'Mme Zoutmans' as the variety is usually spelled nowadays, was another very good damask rose from the same period.

'Mme Hardy': *most beautiful of the old roses.*
OPPOSITE: *'Mme Hardy' makes a shrub 5ft (1.5m) high.*

MADAME ISAAC PEREIRE

It seems likely that 'Mme Isaac Pereire' was named after the wife of one of the Pereire brothers, bankers during the Second Empire in France, when Napoleon III was on the throne. Their financial transactions were, to put it kindly, adventurous, which caused their downfall, but their name lives on in a wonderful member of the bourbon family.

Raised in 1880 by Garçon in Rouen (the parents are unknown) 'Mme Isaac Pereire' is enormously vigorous and has blooms of a size and magnificence to match this vigour, even if, in the first June flush, some can be malformed for reasons that nobody seems fully to understand. However, many of the early ones and, in the autumn all of them, are quite breathtaking, the cool, damper air late in the year seeming to suit them. Probably the most richly scented of all roses, the flowers of 'Mme Isaac Pereire' open cupped, crammed with petals and sometimes quartered, a deep carmine pink with a slightly paler reverse. It is a colour that blends well with other old roses, but needs keeping away from the modern orange and red tones.

Robust is a good word for the growth of this rose and the thick, strong shoots will produce a 7 × 6ft (2.1. × 1.8m) shrub which will greatly benefit from being trained on a tripod or other similar kind of support. It can, as can many of the other bourbons, also be used as a short climber. Large, handsome leaves are an added attraction.

Eight years after its introduction, 'Mme Isaac Pereire' produced a pale pink sport. This occurred in two places, first in the Schwartz nursery in Lyon and, at more or less the same time, in the garden of an Irish priest. It was marketed (and still is) under the name 'Mme Ernst Calvat' and is just as robust a grower as its parent, with attractive red-tinted young leaves. Like 'Mme Isaac Pereire', it really should have some form of support to keep its wayward shoots under control, and it will make a good pillar rose. Its very large double blooms, globular in shape

'Mme Ernst Calvat' is a sport of 'Mme Isaac Pereire' with paler flowers.

Of enormous vigour, 'Mme Isaac Periere' has huge blooms with a strong fragrance.

and often quartered, and with crinkly petals of silvery peach, deepening in the centre to deep rose-pink with a marginally darker reverse, are very pleasing. There is a fine scent and a good autumn showing of blooms.

Both 'Mme Ernst Calvat' and 'Mme Isaac Pereire' can be pegged down in the Victorian fashion, which involves tipping the long shoots in autumn and then tying the ends down to pegs driven into the ground around the plant. This encourages all the flowering side shoots to break into growth and gives a great cushion of bloom in the following year.

Graham Thomas's descriptions of roses are always so evocative that it is difficult to resist quoting him. Here he is about this rose: 'I feel that my choice of the soft carmine-purple 'Madame Isaac Pereire' as one of the most sumptuous and fragrant of all roses will sufficiently cover its attractions; in September its blooms are a model of full-petalled perfection, remaining shapely till they drop.' And David Austin calls it 'a sumptuous beauty, especially when well grown!'

And just to show that I am nothing if not even-handed, here is Jack Harkness: 'This has shaggy double flowers in which strident pink fights a losing battle against the inroads of magenta; from it arose a sport, 'Mme Ernst Calvat', which is more resolute in maintaining its pink identity ... if 'Mme Pierre Oger' is Cinderella, these two are the ugly sisters ... few shrubs can rival their ungainly habit, to avoid which the experts propose they should be grown as climbers; and for a wall facing a neighbour one wishes to annoy, they are ideal subjects.' Truly, one cannot please everybody.

MAIGOLD

Although 'Maigold' is a climber and was raised in Germany by Wilhelm Kordes, it is not, in fact, one of the group known as Kordesii climbers, which includes such varieties as 'Dortmund', 'Hamburger Phoenix', 'Leverkusen', 'Parkdirektor Riggers' and 'Ritter Von Barmstede'. The origination of these goes back to 1941 when Kordes was experimenting with a rose called 'Max Graf' which, with a believed parentage of R. *rugosa* and R. *wichuraiana*, he felt would lead to something very worthwhile that would be both healthy and hardy in the harsh north German winters. Nothing in rose breeding happens overnight, but at length a seedling was produced which, through, a spontaneous chromosome count

Though a modern climber, 'Maigold' has only one main flowering period – in late May.

change from fourteen to twenty-eight, became compatible with the twenty-eight chromosomes of hybrid teas and floribundas and so capable of inter-breeding with them, thus combining the best of both worlds. The new rose proved to come true from seed and thereby achieved the status of a species. It was named after its raiser and became R. *kordesii*.

So successful was the breeding that followed from this that the National Rose Society has hardly yet recovered from the shock of receiving for trial in 1951 over forty hybrids. By no means all of them survived and some, perhaps, did not deserve to, but more of them are still grown in Germany than elsewhere. A number were introduced as hardy climbers but could more accurately be described as vigorous shrubs and not always very elegant ones at that. However, they did achieve a lot of what Herr Kordes had been aiming for – health, freedom of flowering, at least in the first flush and, above all else, great hardiness.

'Maigold', introduced by Kordes at about the same time in 1953, came from a completely different breeding line, though a question mark hangs over exactly what it may have been. Sometimes the parentage is given as 'McGredy's Wonder' (a coppery-orange hybrid tea) × 'Frühlingsgold', which is a pimpinellifolia hybrid. More usually it is stated to be 'Poulsen's Pink' (an early floribunda) × 'Frühlingstag'. *Modern Roses*, usually the 'bible' in which all rose pedigrees can be found, is non-committal and gives both as possible alternatives but, since the parentage of 'Frühlingstag' appears to be 'McGredy's Wonder' × 'Frühlingsgold', I wonder if this is where the confusion has originated. Alas, Herr Kordes is no longer with us to adjudicate. The incredible thorniness of the stems of 'Maigold' do, nevertheless, leave no doubt that the pimpinellifolia group had a hand in its creation, and a very strong pair of gloves is needed to handle it.

The colour of 'Maigold' would certainly lead one to think that 'McGredy's Wonder' was a parent, for the double blooms are reddish in the bud and open to a wonderful deep golden yellow with a hint of copper tones and with golden stamens in the centre. They are richly fragrant.

'Maigold' is one of the earliest roses into flower late in May with a quite breathtaking display, and it is often said that it will not flower again. True,

anything that comes later will not match the early show, but with a certain amount of dead-heading it will certainly, after a brief pause, produce more blooms later in the year. The foliage is first class, a good medium green and glossy, rarely disfigured by fungus attack.

Although a very vigorous grower, 'Maigold' has sometimes been described as more a shrub than a climber. With appropriate moderately hard pruning it can certainly be grown as a shrub and I have used it very effectively in this way to introduce a new colour into a mixed planting. However, against a wall you can expect 15 ft (4.5 m) or so of growth and it will be equally at home on a pillar, arch or pergola, or even climbing, hand-over-hand, up a modest-sized tree.

Though few blooms come after the first flush, the May–June display can be breathtaking.

MARGARET MERRIL

In his book *Roses* Jack Harkness revealed that 'Margaret Merril' was nothing like the rose he hoped to produce when he made the cross. He used a seedling resulting from a union between 'Rudolph Timm' (which has Sweetbrier blood through 'Magnifica') and one of his own roses, the creamy, ivory-white 'Dedication'. This seedling was pink but faded to, of all things, a bright green, and by crossing it in turn with the ivory-white hybrid tea 'Pascali', he hoped it would result in a rose with at least a hint of green. It did not, but later he was to produce the strange-looking 'Greensleeves', so this search for a green rose was a recurring theme.

When 'Margaret Merril' was first introduced in 1977, its scent attracted the attention of the makers of Oil of Ulay and by arrangement with them was named after their beauty counsellor. However, on endeavouring to make contact with the lady, it was discovered that she existed only in the imagination of the Ulay publicity department and was not a real person at all. Since that time three genuine Margaret Merrils have emerged and each is happy to think that this is her very own rose.

That 'Margaret Merril' has made considerable headway in competition with the long-established 'Iceberg' says something for its qualities. It is, however, much more conventional in its habit of growth, being sturdily upright and carrying its flowers in medium-sized trusses mainly at the top of the bush in true floribunda fashion. And what flowers they are! Large, double, but opening wide and flat, they have a cool, satiny look about them. Superficially white, a closer look will detect a blush-pink suffusion and,

when the blooms first open, the stamens are pink too. But above all, what has made this rose such a winner is its rich, sweet fragrance which knocks that of 'Iceberg' quite sideways. To complete the picture fine, glossy, dark green and rather holly-like foliage sets the blooms off to perfection.

If you are looking for faults, one may be found in 'Margaret Merril's lack of resistance to black spot after midsummer, but a systemic rose fungicide will keep that under control. It was certainly not serious enough to prevent the award of a Certificate of Merit and the Edland Medal for fragrance from the RNRS, plus fragrance awards in Monza, New Zealand and The Hague, a Gold Medal in Geneva and the James Mason Memorial Medal, the requirements for which were outlined in the pages describing 'Just Joey', another recipient of this most coveted honour.

Despite the competition already mentioned and the fact that white roses rarely become best-sellers ('Iceberg' always excepted), 'Margaret Merril' has held its head up bravely (perhaps with a touch of smugness that only such a strongly scented floribunda can have) and at the time of writing is in fifth place in order of popularity in the annual Rose Analysis carried out by the RNRS, and that is all of eighteen years after its introduction.

I mentioned, when discussing 'Iceberg', the difficulty that white varieties have in making much headway with the rose-growing public. 'Margaret Merril' has also made the grade, but these two are exceptions and it might be worthwhile to enlarge on the subject a little here. I referred, in the 'Iceberg' piece, to the floribundas 'Ice White' and 'Ivory

The enchanting white blooms of 'Margaret Merril' are sweetly scented.

Fashion', both of which I grew at one time and both of which were good, if conventional, floribundas. They struggled to make an impression for quite a while in the United Kingdom, but neither achieved what they should have done, though 'Ivory Fashion' was more of a success in the United States and much used as an exhibition rose. If asked why I no longer grow them myself, the answer is simple. It is not that they did not do well. The problem is that I write about both old and new roses, and to do this properly one must preferably have grown the roses in question. There is a limit to the number of varieties my garden will hold and, while there are some roses with which I would never willingly part, some do have to go to make room for the new, even though they may be performing perfectly well.

The lack of lasting success for white roses is not, of course, confined to floribundas. Among bedding roses 'Frau Karl Druschki' is a veteran from 1901, still going strong but nowadays kept alive by old rose enthusiasts rather than by the average gardener. In America it is known as 'White American Beauty' and it is sometimes called 'Snow Queen', both in the USA and in the United Kingdom. The latter was a name it acquired during the First World War, when it was considered that a German rose with a name like 'Frau Karl Druschki' was not something that a patriotic Englishman should tip his gardening hat to. But where now are the much more recent 'Virgo', 'Message' ('White Knight'), 'John F. Kennedy', 'Yorkshire Bank', 'White Christmas' and the rest? 'Pascali' is holding on, just about, but it is a very narrow, upright grower with rather small flowers that have a fawn tint in the centre so that they lack the pure whiteness we are looking for. 'Polar Star' is probably the best bet nowadays if one is looking for a white hybrid tea, but it does not even appear in the RNRS Rose Analysis. I find all this sad, for I like white roses, but there it is. Thank goodness for 'Margaret Merril'. Long may she reign.

MORNING JEWEL

Although this book is supposed to contain a selection of fifty roses and their descriptions, I am now going to deviate from this pattern (as those readers of a reasonably high IQ will realize I have been doing with some frequency already) and discuss three roses in some detail under the one heading. My excuse for doing this up to now has been that the varieties described have been linked in some way, usually by family. Here it is a question of three climbing roses, all with 'New Dawn' as one parent and all turning out to be rather similar. This makes it difficult to choose between them, although I have no doubts in my own mind as to which is the best.

'Pink Perpetue' is one of a trio of fine, repeat-flowering, modern climbers.

'Morning Jewel' gets my vote, though not, I must confess, by a very great deal, and it is not altogether easy to explain why. I think it is because it has an extra sparkle that the others lack. With the parentage of 'New Dawn' × 'Red Dandy', it was launched by James Cocker in 1968 at the same time as that other good climber of his, 'Rosy Mantle', which actually did better than 'Morning Jewel' in that it gained a RNRS Trial Ground Certificate. However, neither of them made an immediate impact, probably because 'Pink Perpetue' had preceded them in 1965 and had already a considerable reputation as a reliable pink climber of moderate vigour. This had been followed in 1967 by Sam McGredy's 'Bantry Bay', which came into the same general category.

All three roses have stood up well to the test of time, with 'Pink Perpetue' still top of the three in the nursery lists. Gradually, however, as people realize its worth, 'Morning Jewel' is catching up and it would by no means be the first rose to make a slow start until, gradually, its qualities became recognized by growers.

Like one of its parents, 'New Dawn' (the other was a tall-growing red floribunda), it tends to be a lateral grower and so is ideal for covering a fence or low wall, but it can be quite easily taken up to 10ft (3m) or so on the wall of a house, given a little time to get started. The semi-double flowers are about $3\frac{1}{2}$in (9cm) across and of a glowing, rich pink, at times

OPPOSITE: *'Morning Jewel' is the choicest of the three described here, with an extra sparkle to its deep pink blooms.*

For a good, healthy, modern climber in a paler pink than the others, pick 'Bantry Bay'.

almost luminous. When fully expanded they show an attractive corolla of stamens, and they are beautifully fragrant. Beginning in mid-June, this rose will put on a display that few can better, and there will seldom be a time from then on when it is out of flower. It is always desirable that a climber should produce plentiful basal growth so that a good coverage is given low down and in this 'Morning Jewel' scores well, as it does with its more than ample leaf coverage. This is not a rose with which a low-growing shrub has to be used to cover a bare base. Moreover, the glossy foliage, which will glisten in the sun, is trouble free.

A great deal of what has been said about 'Morning Jewel' could also be used to describe 'Pink Perpetue', which was raised by C. Gregory & Son from 'Danse du Feu' × 'New Dawn', or so the records say; but I believe it was Walter Gregory

himself who said that if you've got a good new rose you can always find two good parents for it. However, the flowers lack character and the colouring is somehow cold. It also needs pretty thorough dead-heading to produce a worthwhile second crop, not always the easiest of things to do on a climber.

'Bantry Bay', the third of our pink climbers, bred from 'New Dawn' and the orange-scarlet, Gold Medal-winning floribunda 'Korona', falls down a little on the question of health in that black spot can be a problem in some years. It will grow rather larger than the other two – up to 12ft (3.5m) on a wall, carrying great clusters of its semi-double flowers with great freedom. They are of a paler pink than those of either 'Pink Perpetue' or 'Morning Jewel'. New clusters will form on basal shoots which come freely throughout the summer, but once again 'Morning Jewel's inner glow is missing.

MUTABILIS

Realizing that the roses in this book are appearing in alphabetical order, and that this is the last rose to appear under the letter 'M', many enthusiasts may wonder what has happened to 'Mermaid'. The answer is, of course, that it may be their favourite but it is not mine. Always, it seems, extravagantly praised, to me it is a rose that has extremely beautiful flowers but never enough of them at any one time. Its health is always extolled but with me it had mildew every year, was not the easiest of roses to train and did not much like pruning to keep it in bounds. However, it is dangerous to be too dismissive of a variety simply because of one's own experi-

'Mutabilis' exhibiting three colour changes as it ages.

ence of it. I once found that out with reference to the yellow rugosa rose 'Agnes', which I had never grown although I had seen it a number of times as a tall, straggly and rather gaunt bush with the minimum of rather washed-out looking flowers. I wrote it off, literally, and then one day – I cannot remember where – I at last saw 'Agnes' as it should be grown, with its sumptuous, double yellow, scented flowers and fine bushy growth. A lesson learned, but how many people had been put off it because of my previous criticism?

However, there can be no doubt about 'Mutabilis', our next rose. Many people, if asked to name a variety the flowers of which opened a coppery-yellow, turning gradually to pink, and which finished up a reddish colour would plump for the floribunda 'Masquerade'. They would be right, of course, but another rose, and a much older one, does much the same thing, though the colours are more pleasing and subtle. This is R. *chinensis* 'Mutabilis', or 'Tipo Ideal' as it used to be called, in which the blooms open from flame-coloured buds to reveal first a soft chamois-yellow colouring within but still with orange-flame on the outside, changing in turn quite rapidly to a soft coppery-pink and finally to a coppery-crimson. There is none of the rather grubby-looking red of the final stages of 'Masquerade'. The flowers are single with waved petals and the plant in full flush resembles nothing so much as a flock of butterflies.

Of unknown age and derivation, it is almost certainly a China rose, one of those brought to the West in the eighteenth century. It is often said that

The multi-colour blooms of 'Mutabilis' have been likened to a flock of butterflies.

Redouté painted a portrait of it, but what he actually shows in his plate is the centifolia 'Unique Blanche', which also went by the name 'Mutabilis' at that time. In fact our rose was given its name comparatively recently by the Swiss alpine gardener Henri Correvon, the man who was also instrumental in reviving interest in *R. rouletii* and thus in all the miniature roses that have descended from it. He was given 'Mutabilis' by Prince Borromeo of the famous garden on Lake Maggiore in northern Italy, and at that time it appeared to be nameless.

'Mutabilis' is not one hundred per cent hardy but thrives with some protection from a warm wall. On this it can be used as a climber, reaching on average about 12ft (3.5m), as it does on the wall of the headquarters building at the Gardens of the Rose. In exceptional circumstances, however, as on the wall of Kiftsgate Court in Gloucestershire, it has reached all of 50ft (15m). Otherwise it forms a 3–4ft (1–1.2m) well-branched, spreading bush with fine, dark bronze-green leaves. These form a fitting backdrop for the truly remarkable flowers which are carried from early summer until the last months of the year. Single and about 3in (8cm) across, they are borne in clusters, all three stages of their colouring being visible at one time. The bush will look fine in a mixed planting and, if you want a plant to impress visitors, this is it, though some may take a little convincing that it is a rose at all. It can, of course, also be used as a bedding rose where, because of the spread of each plant, one does not need to buy too many of them. That makes it economical as well as beautiful.

The flame-like colouring of the flowers' second stage is what leaves the greatest impression and is not, among China roses, confined to 'Mutabilis'. It can be found in the scented semi-double blooms of 'Comtesse du Cayla', and in 'Mme Laurette Messimy', both of which also change in colour as they age (a characteristic of China roses in general). In few is the colour stable, the pale pinks of many varieties turning to a much deeper pink in hot sunshine, something that has been handed down to a number of modern roses that have Chinese rose blood not too far back in their pedigrees.

NEVADA

This has been for long one of the most popular shrub roses and it is not difficult to see why. It will mix equally well with both old and new roses from whatever period and at its peak of flowering could be said to bear more of its large, semi-double, creamy white flowers than it knows what to do with. They literally cover what will be a large bush, perhaps 6 × 7ft (1.8 × 2.1m), with only an occasional leaf being able to peep through between them. Not surprisingly, however, in view of the effort that must go into this spectacular start at midsummer, there is not a second flush to match the first – just a few flowers to be seen every month and a late, smaller spurt of bloom, not on new shoots thrown up from the base, but from short side shoots on the old branches.

'Nevada' was bred by the Spanish hybridist Pedro Dot, who introduced it in 1927 as a hybrid between his own hybrid tea, the very strong-growing 'La Giralda' and *R. moyesii*. Most authorities hold that *R. moyesii* 'Fargesii' is the most likely second parent, though Jack Harkness, having tried with very little success to breed something worthwhile from *R. moyesii*, suggested that it was more likely that it was *R. pimpinellifolia* 'Hispida'. The debate surfaces anew every so often, but it does not seem that we shall ever have the problem properly resolved, which is a pity when one considers that the rose is such an interesting one.

The leaves of 'Nevada' could be said to show some influence from the *moyesii* strain, in that they are noticeably more rounded than those of most roses. They cover the shrub well (when, that is, they can be seen) and seem mildew proof, though black spot can be a problem. The branches on which they grow are very nearly thornless. In hot weather there can be a pink tinge to many of the flowers, but in the United Kingdom the sun is not usually of a strength to cause this to happen until the first flush is over.

It is not unusual, after perhaps ten years or so, to see a bush of 'Nevada' appearing rather ragged and untidy, looking as if it were past its best and possibly on its way out altogether. This can be prevented from happening quite easily by removing some of the main shoots every few years, cutting them right

A modern shrub of uncertain parentage, 'Nevada' carries its white flowers in great profusion.

At times 'Nevada' will be completely hidden beneath its massed blooms.

to the base to encourage new ones to take their place. Alternatively, if this has not been done regularly, the rose will be rejuvenated by cutting it back really hard in winter, to within 2–3ft (60–90cm) of the ground. In spring it will bounce back, but normally it is not a rose that requires any pruning other than the removal of dead wood as and when it occurs.

'Marguerite Hilling' is a pink sport of 'Nevada' and, like it, makes a large, spreading shrub.

In the 1950s pink sports of 'Nevada' appeared in several places, among them in Sunningdale Nursery near Bagshot in the county of Surrey and in Mrs Nancy Steen's garden in New Zealand; and the rose was first put on the market as 'Marguerite Hilling' by Hillings Nurseries near Farnham, likewise in Surrey. Many people rate it above 'Nevada' but this may just be the natural preference of so many people for a pink rose over a white, for really there is very little difference between them except for their colour. It is sometimes said that 'Marguerite Hilling' is even more floriferous than 'Nevada', but I doubt there is anyone who has counted blooms to make this a statement based on fact. Personally I prefer the white rose, but now and then one can have the best of both worlds when an odd branch of 'Nevada' decides to surprise you with pink blooms – really pink, I mean, and not just those tinted by the sun.

'Nevada' obtained an Award of Merit in 1949 and a First Class Certificate from the Royal Horticultural Society, and 'Marguerite Hilling' an Award of Merit in 1960. I know of no other case where both a rose and its sport have been given the same accolade. The Royal National Rose Society would doubtless also have honoured both roses if they had ever been submitted for trial at St Albans.

THE NEW DAWN

Normally known simply as 'New Dawn', this rose has an interesting and unusual history and, as a breeding parent, still a considerable future. Back in 1910 the distinguished American rose breeder, Dr Walter Van Fleet, who had earlier raised the rambler 'American Pillar', produced another winner. This was also a once-flowering rambler with pale, blush-pink flowers which he named 'Day-break', but when it was put on the market the man who was actually selling it changed the name to 'Dr W. Van Fleet' in honour of the raiser. Some sort of name change would probably have been necessary in any case as another *wichuraiana* hybrid called 'Day-break' had been put on sale by Eastern Nurseries of Massachusetts a year earlier and there was, in ad-dition, Joseph Pemberton's hybrid musk 'Day-break', dating back to 1918.

Not everyone was immediately won over by the new rose. Of it G.A. Stevens, one-time Secretary of the American Rose Society, was to say: 'I approach this rose with awe and humility, although I have never liked it very much. The colour is a wishy-washy pink, characterless and flat, but its influence has been stupendous. Its introduction broke the garden thralldom to innumerable fussy little cluster-flower ramblers which bore us to distraction with their infantile prettiness and indistinguishable differ-ences. Here was an heroic rose, to perfect size and perfect form, borne on a rampant plant, first of a new race of climber.' Others thought more highly of its colouring than Mr Stevens and liked its large, hybrid tea-style flowers. It became immensely popular, which led to a most unexpected development.

During the 1920s, Somerset Rose Nurseries of New Brunswick, New Jersey, was enthusiastically promoting and selling large numbers of the new rose, but with a recession approaching, times became hard. There was an overstock of 'Dr W. Van Fleet' at the end of the season, and in the hope that there would be a quick return to prosperity, they were left in the ground so that they could be sold during the following season. By then, however, 'Buddy can you spare a dime?' was the song of the moment and it was decided that in the fall the crop would be ploughed in. While this was happening, however, one plant was seen to be flowering well after its usual time and a keen-eyed nurseryman spotted its potential. In 1930 this repeat-flowering sport of 'Dr W. Van Fleet' was launched on to the market by Henry A. Dreer of Philadelphia and given the name 'Everblooming Dr W. Van Fleet'. Later this was changed to 'The New Dawn' and it became the first holder of a plant patent as the act protecting new varieties had come into effect in the same year.

America was the only country to recognize that a man who had spent something like eight years breed-ing and then putting on the market a new rose was entitled to some recompense from others who also wanted to grow and sell it. Until 1930 anyone could take bud-wood from a new variety and market the resulting plants without paying a cent to the man who had done all the work in raising it. The act was a start, and eventually there was progress made in other countries. In 1955 the Fourteenth International Horticultural Congress at Scheveningen in Holland established the International Registration Authority

One of the best of all-purpose climbers, 'New Dawn' is parent to many other fine varieties.

for Roses. This is administered by the American Rose Society and among its many functions its register prevents the duplication of variety names. It was not, however, until 1964, with the introduction of the Plant Variety and Seeds Act and with it the Plant Breeders' Rights (Roses) Scheme, that the rights of rose breeders in the United Kingdom received any sort of protection. Now, for a period of twenty years, a royalty must be paid to the raiser by anyone selling stock of a new variety that has been recorded with the Registration Authority.

Coming back to 'New Dawn', there can be few nurseries stocking climbing roses that do not have it in their catalogues. It has for long been one of the best general purpose climbers there is, enchanting all who see it with its soft pink, satiny, scented blooms. It can be grown as a climber in almost any situation and its shoots are flexible enough for training over arches or pergolas, or for making an effective weeping standard. I have seen it grown up a tree to a height of 20ft (6m) or so (though it is probably best trained laterally on a fence), and I have seen it grown by the side of Lake Maggiore in Italy to make a stunning hedge. Or again it can make a free-standing

shrub if started off over a frame of some sort, after which it will mound up on its own.

After the first flush it will produce some flowers throughout the summer with an increase again in early autumn. Harry Wheatcroft, that great rosarian and nurseryman, seems to have been alone in maintaining that it flowered best on the old wood so that pruning should be sparing, but whether or not he was right, the advice he gave was sound for practically any climber. He, incidentally, was one of those who campaigned tirelessly for plant breeders' rights, though he was not, himself, a hybridist.

One aspect of 'New Dawn', which some would say was the most important, has not yet been touched upon, and that is its use in the breeding of other first-class roses. One way or another, either in the first or second generation, 'New Dawn' figures in the parentage of 'Aloha', 'Bantry Bay', 'Compassion', 'City Girl', 'Dublin Bay', 'Étude', 'Highfield', 'High Hopes', 'Morning Jewel', 'Parade', 'Pink Perpetue', 'Rosy Mantle' and 'White Cockade'. And through the pollen of the climber 'Compassion' some fine bush roses have been bred, notably the superlative hybrid tea 'Paul Shirville'.

OFFICINALIS

The variety 'Officinalis' is a gallica rose and the gallicas are the only family from among the old garden roses that is entitled to be written without the '×' indicating hybrid origin. All the others should appear as follows: R. × *damascena*, R. × *alba*, R. × *centifolia*, R. × *centifolia muscosa* (for the moss roses) and R. × *borboniana* for the bourbons. If you include the China rose among the old garden types, the name should be written R. *chinensis* (or R. *sinensis*), the important point being that both R. *gallica* and R. *chinensis* are species in their own right. The damasks, albas, centifolias, moss roses and bourbons are all descendants of the gallica, and the gallica 'Officinalis' is the oldest cultivated rose we know. It appears to be a native of southern France and other countries bordering the northern shores of the Mediterranean, and the wild form is thought to be the rose in a fresco on the wall of the royal palace in Knossos on Crete. R. × *sancta*, the holy rose from Abyssinia, which the ancient Egyptians, at least in their later period, probably knew, is also a form of gallica.

'Officinalis' makes a vigorous, fairly upright shrub about 3–4ft (1–1.2m) tall with only its rather slender outer shoots spreading sideways under the weight of the flowers. These, about 2½in (6cm) in diameter and semi-double, are mostly carried well above the foliage and are of a fiery crimson-pink with pale yellow stamens. They will give a quite dazzling display, though at midsummer only, which means that it is really best if the bush is planted so that it mingles with others, for the rather rough gallica foliage does not age particularly well and mildew can be unsightly from July onward unless spraying is regularly carried out. Other shrubs will distract the eye from this, but even with its mildew, this is a rose I would not want to be without. It will make a really spectacular low hedge, and so will its sport, 'Rosa Mundi'. This is identical in growth but the flowers are of the palest blush-pink, striped with several deeper tones of pink.

'Officinalis' is probably our oldest cultivated variety.

At least part of the fascination of growing 'Officinalis' is in its historical associations. From the Middle Ages onward, it was much grown in France (hence the name 'gallica') as a medicinal plant and for use in the preparation of conserves. Vast fields of it were harvested near the town of Provins, south-east of Paris, which resulted in it being called the Provins rose or Rose of Provins already touched on in the description of 'Fantin-Latour' on page 53. In England the First Earl of Lancaster had a French wife with properties in the Provins area and it is said that he brought the rose across the English Channel and made it his badge. Thus it became the Red Rose of Lancaster, featured in the Wars of the Roses. After the war was over, the house of York with its white (alba) rose and the house of Lancaster with its red 'Officinalis' were joined together under Henry Tudor, as previously recounted (page 10).

The original gallica rose from which all others are descended, photographed in the wild.

OPPOSITE: *The old herbalists used 'Officinalis' in medicines, naming it the Apothecary's Rose.*

'Rosa Mundi' is a striped sport of 'Officinalis' named, it is said, after Fair Rosamund.

For a long time, because of its many medicinal uses, 'Officinalis' was also known as the Apothecary's Rose, as infusions made from its petals, leaves and roots were considered in the distant past to be cures for almost any disease from migraine to measles. A very large proportion of plants in those early days were considered only as herbs and grown as such to a large extent in monastery gardens. Roses, of course, were among them and it is unlikely that many were grown purely for their beauty. Most were for medicines, so the monks had the best of both worlds.

'Rosa Mundi', first recorded about 1580, is said to have been named for Fair Rosamund, the mistress of Henry II, but as his dates are 1154–89, one must, with considerable reluctance, admit that this can hardly be true. Both it and 'Officinalis' require thinning out rather than conventional pruning, and the odd extra-vigorous shoots cut back in winter, as the centres of the bushes can easily become a tangle of twigs. When grown as a hedge, either rose can be gently clipped over with shears, though not to shape it formally like a beech or privet hedge. Think of it as being given a trim at the barber rather than a complete new styling.

PAUL SHIRVILLE

The rose 'Paul Shirville' has been described by a professional photographer as 'the most photogenic rose I know' and few would quarrel with that. It has the most beautiful, shapely blooms, not over large, and mostly carried in small clusters, their colour a blend of salmon-pink and peach tones, shading to yellow at the base of the petals. They combine elegance and substance, for the petals are robust enough to give a good resistance to rain.

Introduced in 1983, it had already gained a Certificate of Merit and a Henry Edland Memorial Medal for fragrance in the Royal National Rose Society's trials, and it is one of the most sweetly scented roses there is. This probably derives from one of its parents, the climber 'Compassion', and its freedom of flowering will have come from the other, Sam McGredy's 'Mischief'.

Many of the other good qualities of 'Compassion' can be recognized in 'Paul Shirville', not least its fine, glossy, dark green leaves. It is a fairly spreading grower and will reach $2\frac{1}{2}$–3ft (75–90cm) in height, making it ideal for bedding, except for one thing: it is almost certain to need watching for black spot in the second half of the year, though the regular use of a systemic rose fungicide spray should keep this in check. Whether or not black spot invades 'Paul Shirville' bushes overseas (where it has an alternative name of 'Heart Throb') I do not know but, if it does, this has not prevented it from carrying off awards for excellence in both New Zealand and Japan. To me, 'Heart Throb' would have been a better name for this rose in the United Kingdom as well as abroad, but this must remain a matter of opinion for the rose was named by his friends for a noted design engineer as a retirement present.

When the Edland Medal and Certificate of Merit awards were announced in the 1983 Rose Annual, 'Paul Shirville' was described as cluster flowered (floribunda/hybrid tea type). The latter part of this description was the rather clumsy term then used to describe a floribunda that had rather larger flowers than was usual, but not large enough to make the rose a hybrid tea. In America the equivalent and much more satisfactory term was grandiflora, but whatever it was called, this rose was in fact half-way between the two, due to the mingling of hybrid tea and floribunda strains by hybridists. Nowadays, however, 'Paul Shirville' has changed its spots and is sold as a hybrid tea, which it would seem it really is. It is an excellent example of the difficulties to be encountered when trying to make a sensible classification for the rose family. Roses, quite simply, do not fit into the slots we allocate for them, even if we know their breeding; and deciding on the parentage of most of the old varieties can be compared with attempting the same task, in a human context, during the ninth century, nine months or so after a Viking raid – a choice of infinite possibilities.

OPPOSITE: *'Paul Shirville' carries so many blooms some call it a floribunda, some a hybrid tea.*

PEACE

It is fashionable nowadays in certain quarters to be rather patronizing about 'Peace' and the reason for this is an age-old one. If something becomes popular with all and sundry, it loses its appeal for the 'discerning'. However, a rose that for over fifty years to date has stood out above all others and which, after forty-seven of those fifty was voted by an international panel to be the World's Favourite Rose, must, I feel, have something.

It is so well known that a description of its qualities would seem superfluous. The picture on this page can speak for it more eloquently than I could, but the story behind its introduction is worth telling, even in outline. Anyone wanting a fuller version is referred to Antonia Ridge's book *For Love of a Rose*, which is entirely devoted to the story of 'Peace' and of the Meilland family who raised it.

It all began in 1935 with a pale yellow seedling under the code name 3-35-40 in the Meilland nursery at Antibes in the south of France. It was picked out for development and, when plants had been budded on to understocks, was by 1939 attracting considerable interest among potential distributors, both from France and overseas. Orders were placed, but distributors do not take whole plants from the raiser of a new variety. They take what is known as budwood, which consists of strong shoots from which buds can be cut for subsequent grafting on to rootstocks by the recipient. Budwood of the new rose (which was as yet unnamed) was sent to Germany and Italy, though not to England as there was no regular distributor for Meilland roses to handle it at that time.

There has never been another rose like 'Peace', voted again and again the World's Favourite Rose.

As for the United States, the story goes that the American ambassador to France was visiting the Meillands when the German invasion of the country had already begun. He was shown the new rose and asked if it could be bought in his own country. He was told that this would only be possible if some way could be found for budwood to be sent to America despite the confusion that the invasion had brought in its wake. That was enough for the ambassador, and budwood left shortly afterwards in the diplomatic bag of the American consul in Lyon.

Meanwhile the rose was being distributed to nurseries in Germany and Italy. In France it went out as 'Mme A. Meilland' in memory of the raiser's wife, but such a name would not do for countries with which France was at war. The rose became 'Gloria Dei' in Germany and 'Gioia' in Italy, while it was in America that the name 'Peace' was chosen by the Conard Pyle Company, who had the rights of distribution there. They realized that they had a great rose on their hands, with flowers bigger and more glorious than any other hybrid tea; and the time was right, with the ending of the war, for a rose with such

a name. In 1945 they launched it and, not long afterwards, at a meeting of the newly created United Nations in San Francisco, each delegate had placed in his hotel room by the American Rose Society a single bloom of 'Peace' with an inscription which read: 'This is the Peace rose which was christened at the Pacific Rose Society exhibition in Pasadena on the day Berlin fell. We hope that the Peace rose will influence men's thoughts for everlasting world peace.'

It was 1947 before it could be sold in Great Britain, but when it was launched there it carried

The huge, pale yellow blooms of 'Peace' have won many awards at rose shows world-wide.

proudly with it a Gold Medal of the Royal National Rose Society, only one in a long line of awards that were to come from numerous other countries.

Since that time 'Peace' has been used very extensively in breeding and has handed on many of its good qualities to later varieties. Nowadays the influence is still there, though much diluted through intermingling with other strains; but notable roses that came early on and had relatively close links with 'Peace' were 'Rose Gaujard', 'Karl Herbst', 'Pink Peace', 'Michèle Meilland', 'Grand'mère Jenny', 'Stella' and 'Gold Crown'. There were a number of sports, too, although only two made much of an impact. These were the bicolour 'Kronenburg' and 'Chicago Peace'; the latter takes its name from the town where it was first discovered and is 'Peace' in duplicate, but with flowers in rich blends of pink, light yellow and orange. There is also a climbing sport of 'Peace', but those living in a climate like that of the United Kingdom would do well to steer clear. I planted one and kept it for four years, during which time it produced almost unlimited growth and just one flower. I have since learned that this is not untypical, although I have seen pictures of it doing pretty well in hotter climes. For those who wish to know more about the roses on which 'Peace' has had an influence, even now Dick Balfour, a Past President of the RNRS, is establishing at the Gardens of the Rose a series of beds featuring varieties with 'Peace' in their family trees. The total number is quite staggering.

Just what was it that gave 'Peace' its great infusion of vigour? It is said that the introduction of a species into the breeding lines of a rose will do this, and the first published family tree of 'Peace' showed a descent from the 'Austrian Copper', R. *foetida*

'Chicago Peace' is a sport of 'Peace'. The possibly unstable colour of a sport is well shown in the picture.

'Bicolor'. This was based on information supplied by the Meilland family, but there must be some doubt that the nursery records were accurate. There is absolutely no sign of the influence of the 'Austrian Copper' in 'Peace' or any of its offspring, so that another version of the pedigree, also claimed to be from the Meilland records, is a more likely one and reads as shown in the family tree below.

All good roses these, and all could have played their part, but for the total result to have added up to 'Peace' the unpredictability element that plays so large a part in rose breeding must have been a major factor.

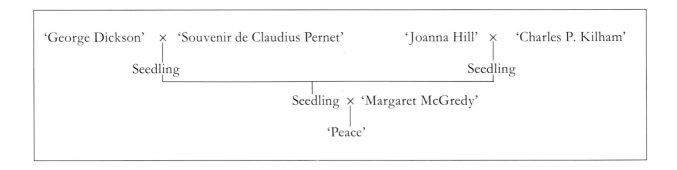

'George Dickson' × 'Souvenir de Claudius Pernet'   'Joanna Hill' × 'Charles P. Kilham'

Seedling   Seedling

Seedling × 'Margaret McGredy'

'Peace'

PRISTINE

When writing on page 14 about 'Aloha', I said a little about the difficulty in finding roses that will do equally well on both sides of the Atlantic. 'Pristine' is one that has sailed triumphantly across from west to east, making itself very much at home and gaining a Certificate of Merit and an Edland Medal for Fragrance in the RNRS trials, after winning a Portland Gold Medal at home.

I also enlarged elsewhere on the scarcity of good white roses, especially among the hybrid teas. 'Pristine' was not mentioned then because, though when viewed from a distance it may appear white, I do not really think of it as a white rose. The centres of the strongly fragrant blooms are ivory-white, shading to pale blush at the edges of the truly enormous petals. High-centred at first, the flowers open out fairly quickly and certainly an exhibitor of blinkered vision would say that a few extra petals, over and above the existing eighteen, would be an advantage. I disagree, for, even when fully opened out, the blooms are of extreme beauty, the petals attractively waved. More, and its whole character would be changed.

The flowers, carried sometimes singly and sometimes in clusters of three or four, are given a wonderful background by the very large, dark green leaves. The plant itself is very robust, sending up strong shoots to about $3\frac{1}{2}$ft (1.1m) which makes it on the tall side for bedding. Disease quite passes it by.

'Pristine' was raised by W.A. Warriner and introduced by Jackson & Perkins in the USA in 1978. The parents were two hybrid teas, 'White Masterpiece', and a great American show rose called 'First Prize' which was an All American Rose selection.

Bearing the most exquisite blooms, 'Pristine' is a strong grower, rather tall for bedding.

'Pristine', an American rose, does well in the UK.

QUEEN ELIZABETH

The rose 'Queen Elizabeth' was raised by Dr W.E. Lammerts in America from a cross between another rose of his raising, the blood-red hybrid tea 'Charlotte Armstrong', and the red floribunda 'Floradora' from Tantau in Germany. It was introduced in 1954 by Germain's Nursery of Los Angeles and by Harry Wheatcroft in the United Kingdom. Reminiscing, Harry would love to tell how he had, for a number of years, seen it blooming under trial all across the United States and how thrilled he was to introduce in the UK.

As one of the world's greatest roses there was little surprise when it easily gained an RNRS Gold Medal and a Gold Medal and Golden Rose Award at The Hague. It was also an All American Rose Selection but almost missed out on this, though not through lack of quality. When first put forward it was described as a hybrid tea, and as such was greeted with no great enthusiasm. It gained few points as it was considered too tall and ungainly. However, although clearly it would not qualify as a hybrid tea, it was equally obviously an outstanding variety which seemed to be being brushed aside because it did not fit some preconceived pattern. Common sense prevailed and a completely new class was created especially for it, so that it became the first of what were to be known as grandifloras, a term, incidentally, hardly recognized outside the United States. 'Queen Elizabeth' was, in its new guise, re-entered in the All American trials and came out a winner. In the United Kingdom it is a floribunda, although it no more resembles a typical rose of that class than it does a hybrid tea. It is unique.

Officially a floribunda, the blooms of 'Queen Elizabeth' are larger than most of the class.

Fine rose though it is, 'Queen Elizabeth' can easily become odd man out in the garden if care is not taken to plant it in the right spot. Very tall and upright, it can exceed 8ft (2.4m), with its flowers mainly very high up. Nevertheless, it can be restrained to some extent and persuaded to bush out more by what might be called differential pruning. Do not, in other words, treat all the shoots with equal severity, but cut back a few hard each year and others much less drastically. Even with this treatment, however, 'Queen Elizabeth' will never

OPPOSITE: *An exceptionally tall grower, a good place for 'Queen Elizabeth' is the back of the border.*

Its height makes 'Queen Elizabeth' an ideal hedging rose.

become a bedding rose. It can, on the other hand, be used most effectively for the back of the border, whether this contains other roses only or is a mixed planting, for its soft, china-pink colouring will blend most happily with anything you care to plant near it. Or it can be used with great effect as a hedging rose, probably best not arranged in single file but using two staggered planting lines, each bush about 3½ft (1.1m) from its neighbour. With the kind of pruning advocated there should be a good coverage of leaves quite low down and, as they are of a deep, glossy green and almost disease proof, they are an added attraction.

In a hedge, as elsewhere, the large, cupped blooms, carried sometimes singly but more often in sizeable trusses, will still be mainly at the top, but with judicious trimming they can be kept down to little more than 5ft (1.5m). The long flower stems are almost thornless – a great advantage when cutting for the house – and flowers last very well in water. Pretty well weatherproof, they lack only scent to put them in the very highest class. As a show rose 'Queen Elizabeth' has carried off top prizes again and again. There is a climbing sport of 'Queen Elizabeth', which I have heard of but never seen. I cannot imagine why it was necessary.

RAMBLING RECTOR

Once you have seen great waterfalls of bloom from a climbing or rambling rose cascading down from the branches of a tall tree, it is unlikely that you will be able to rest until you have something similar in your own garden. It is one of the most breathtaking sights and, with varieties from the multiflora family, there will be scent wafting on the air as well. However, it is not sufficient to plant any old climber at the foot of any old tree and hope for the best. The growing of such a rose does need some thought; there are certain questions which should be answered before you begin.

Assuming that you realize that a really vigorous rose is needed, the first thing to be decided is not which variety of rose to use but whether or not you have a suitable tree available. It should, for instance, be well branched fairly low down so that there is support for the shoots in their early stages of growth. A Scots pine, with its long, bare stem going up perhaps 20ft (6m) before branching starts, would present difficulties. A holly or an apple tree, on the other hand, would be quite suitable, though only for a moderately vigorous rose such as 'New Dawn', 'Blush Rambler' or 'Sander's White'. Such a tree might, in an incredibly short time, be overwhelmed by a rose such as 'Rambling Rector', which really requires one that is not only well-branched but also of herculean strength. The weight of a 'Rambling Rector' and others of its kind when fully grown, plus the added wind resistance from its leaves, may just about double the load the tree trunk has to bear, so that the chosen tree (even for a considerably smaller rose) must be sound in wind and limb. An ancient

'Rambling Rector' has numerous small, semi-double flowers.

apple tree may, on the face of it, look ideal because its own leaves are becoming rather sparse and the gaps left need filling, but it may be a good deal more frail than it looks. With the added burden of the rose, the winter gales may bring the tree crashing down, and what has to be faced in untangling such a disaster can only be fully realized by someone like myself, who has actually had to do it through not following his own advice.

'Rambling Rector' can be a tree-climbing rose but also looks well on a wall.

For a tall tree there are quite a number of white climbers and ramblers with huge heads of small white flowers which you can choose from, and 'Rambling Rector' would be a good one to start with. It has the added attraction of a name with a nice, Victorian ring to it, although in fact it first appeared in a grower's catalogue (the Daisy Hill Nursery in Northern Ireland) in 1912. No parentage has ever been established, but it is clearly closely related to *R. multiflora*. Its flowers are, however, semi-double, creamy white on first opening, then quickly fading to white, the yellow stamens losing their colour fairly rapidly, though this is hardly noticeable on a rose with blooms that are mostly viewed from a considerable distance. In full flower their numbers have to be seen to be believed.

Freely branching, it can also be used to scramble through and over a hedge or to hide an old shed, but on a tree it will easily reach 20ft (6m) or more, weaving its way up with the greatest facility. It does this by sending new 5–6ft (1.5–1.8m) side shoots vertically upward from older ones which have curved over under their own weight, and this process is repeated over and over again as the rose gains hold.

Having established that, for 'Rambling Rector', you need both a large and a strong tree, it must be added that it should also be situated in the right spot. If it is on the southern boundary of your garden, your neighbour will see more of the rose in bloom than you will yourself. Rose shoots, seeking the sun, will gradually work their way through to the southern side of the tree, and that is where their flowers will be. Plant your 'Rambling Rector' about 6–7ft (1.8–2.1m) away from the tree trunk so that it will stand a better chance in competition with the tree roots, both for nutrients and for water. Train it in toward the tree trunk along a rope anchored to a peg in the ground beside the rose, or along a pole or cane. Once the shoots begin to hook themselves on the lower branches of the tree, the rose can to a large extent be left to make its way upward. It does help, however, if it has been planted on the windward side of the tree, as the prevailing wind will tend to blow the shoots in toward the tree and not out of it.

Pruning will not be needed and would, in any case, be just about impossible, which will delight anyone thinking of growing roses in this way for the first time. The climbers, and even more so the ramblers, generally used for tree-climbing are, if not species themselves, mostly hybrids of species and thus very close to their wild ancestors. In climbing through trees they are growing very much as they do in nature when, of course, they get neither sprayed for disease nor pruned. They thrive nevertheless, and old, worn-out wood dies away naturally in the treetops as new shoots take its place. This happens rather more slowly than it does with carefully tended garden roses, but pruning is, after all, simply a means of speeding up a natural sequence. As far as diseases and insect pests are concerned, an enormously vigorous plant such as 'Rambling Rector' can more or less shrug them off.

Roses of the 'Rambling Rector' kind have many uses. Here it is a free-standing shrub.

ROSERAIE DE L'HAÿ

A most wonderful shrub and perhaps the best of all roses for making a colourful hedge. It will grow to about 6ft (1.8m) tall, branching freely but keeping reasonably upright, and covered right to the ground with its lush green, deeply veined and completely disease-free leaves, which change colour briefly to yellow before they fall in autumn. Its flowers, coming in small clusters from shapely, scrolled buds, appear early in June and from then onward there will scarcely be a time when the bush is without at least a few, though there are two main flushes. The colour of the sweetly scented flowers is a rich crimson-purple, and they open wide to show creamy-yellow stamens but, as this is a rugosa rose with double blooms, they are not followed by the usual striking hips.

'Roseraie de l'Haÿ' will make big bushes, so for a hedge they should be planted about 4ft (1.2m) apart, when they will grow to form a dense screen, rendered almost intruder-proof by their extremely thorny (prickly) stems. I have put prickly in brackets but, to be botanically accurate, it is strictly the correct word. Although few gardeners refer to anything other than thorns when talking of roses, this name should properly be given to the spines found on blackthorn and gorse, sharp, straight and pointed, actually modified branches. The random prickles on rose stems are superficial growths arising from the bark cells, may come in many forms, and can easily be snapped off as the shoot ripens. To remove a thorn it would have to be cut away.

'Roseraie de l'Haÿ' needs little attention from the secateurs but will benefit from having one or more of its main shoots cut right back every few years to encourage new growth from lower down the plant.

A little was said about the history of R. *rugosa* when we were dealing with 'Fru Dagmar Hastrup' on page 58. This might be the place to expand on it a little, for it is a very ancient rose of considerable interest. A native of Korea, Japan and northern China, it is said to have been cultivated since AD1100 in China, where pot-pourri was prepared from its petals. There were the same colour forms as exist today, ranging from white through pink to crimson. Mostly it grew in sandy soils near the sea, and it was first described for Western readers by Thunberg in 1784. He used the name Ramanas Rose, which Bean suggests is probably a slip of the pen or a mishearing, for it should actually be 'Hama-nashi', which in Japanese means 'shore-pear', emphasizing the fact that the rose will put up with poor, sandy soils – a useful quality not to be forgotten today by gardeners who live near the sea.

It was first cultivated in Britain toward the end of the eighteenth century, growing under the name R. *ferox*, but made no great impact. It was not until it was reintroduced around 1870 that it really came to gardeners' attention, the more so when genuinely worthwhile and garden-worthy hybrids began to appear, for R. *rugosa* itself is not a particularly exciting plant. This was at the turn of the century and they included 'Blanc Double de Coubert' (1892), 'Belle Poitevine' and 'Souvenir de Christoph

OPPOSITE: *The rugosa 'Roseraie de l'Haÿ' is one of the best hedging roses, healthy and floriferous.*

Cochet', both of 1894, and 'Souvenir de Philemon Cochet' of 1899, together with two from America, 'Delicata' (1898) and 'Hansa' (1905). 'Roseraie de l'Haÿ' is of this period, too, probably a hybrid of R. *rugosa* 'Rubra' rather than a sport of R. *rugosa* 'Rosea', as has sometimes been suggested. It is credited to M. Jules Gravereaux, the moving spirit behind the rose gardens at l'Haÿ and Bagatelle, but was actually introduced by those breeders of other good rugosas, Messrs Cochet-Cochet. Do not confuse it with 'Rose à Parfum de l'Haÿ' when ordering, for the latter, though superficially not unlike it, is but a sorry thing in comparison.

Very few hybrids of R. *rugosa* were produced in the years that followed, but recently, with resistance to disease being considered more and more important, breeders have woken up to the fact that here is a rose family that can perhaps show the way. Some worthwhile new rugosas have begun to appear, notably varieties like 'Jens Munk' and 'Martin Frobisher' from Canada, where breeding for hardiness as well as health has been a factor. 'Robusta' came in recent years from Germany and an enormously promising newcomer is 'Pierette', though this variety is still under trial.

'Robusta' is a modern rugosa hybrid from Germany, showing few family characteristics.

Hardy roses are needed in Canada. 'Jens Munk' was raised there.

ROYAL WILLIAM

No rose selection would be complete without its deep, dusky red, strongly scented hybrid tea and, in making a decision as to which one I should include, my feelings were divided between my final choices, 'Royal William' and 'Ingrid Bergman'. 'Royal William' just got the vote because it is more strongly scented.

In general, as I have already indicated, I do not go along with those who hold that modern roses have lost their scent, but I must agree that, with the deep red varieties, this seems, regrettably, to be true. One looks, perhaps with undue nostalgia, back to the 1930s and 'Étoile de Hollande' and 'Crimson Glory', or to the 1950s which gave us 'Charles Mallerin', 'Karl Herbst', 'Chrysler Imperial', 'Josephine Bruce' and 'Mme Louis Laperrière'; yet since that time, although there have been plenty of excellent deep red roses, those that were strongly scented have been few and far between. 'Mister Lincoln' came in 1964 with a good scent, but it was a leggy, ungainly grower rather lacking in petals so that it opened very quickly. 'My Love' was of about the same date and had a good fragrance. But what has there been since?

Nowadays one can find a few, among them 'Royal William', about which more will be said shortly. Then there is 'Deep Secret', but its flowers are usually poorly formed and burn black in the sun. 'John Waterer' is a fragrant rose and a good one, too, but somehow never really caught on and is nowadays only obtainable at a very few nurseries. Of the rest (though this does not claim to be a completely comprehensive list) 'Ingrid Bergman', 'Big Chief',

The blooms of 'Royal William' are always immaculate and the plant vigorous and healthy.

'Malcolm Sargent', 'Loving Memory' and 'Precious Platinum' all come under the heading of 'some fragrance'. Also there is the otherwise excellent 'National Trust', in which it is impossible to detect any scent at all.

I am not advocating growing 'Crimson Glory' nowadays or 'Étoile de Hollande', which tended to have rather sparse foliage, although the latter may still be worth having in its climbing form. 'Crimson Glory' deteriorated badly toward the end of its useful life and one tends only to remember the best of other old varieties, for most of these unfortunately also had faults.

Towards the end of summer 'Royal William' will send up large clusters of smaller blooms.

And so we move back to 'Royal William', also known as 'Duftzauber 84' and 'Fragrant Charm 84', which was bred in Germany by the Kordes nursery and introduced ten years ago. This would appear to have been before it had finished its trials at the Rose Society, for it did not receive a Trial Ground Certificate until 1985, which is by no means unusual. If a grower is quite certain he has a winner on his hands, he will launch it on the market without waiting for trial results other than those he may have carried out himself. If awards come later, it is a bonus and, in the case of 'Royal William', they did. In addition, 'Royal William' became the British Rose of the Year 1987.

It is a very sturdy grower, sending up strong shoots that will take it up to $3-3\frac{1}{2}$ft (1–1.1m), making it on the tall side for bedding, at least in a small bed. The blooms are a deep crimson, fragrant and shapely, carried sometimes one to a stem but more often in clusters of up to six, so that some disbudding would be needed if they are to be used for showing. In the autumn, on a few shoots, the clusters become even larger, heads of seven to eight flowers being not uncommon, putting on a very fine display as they are well spread out in the truss and do not crowd one another. This is a familiar phenomenon, as floribun-

das and hybrid teas reverse roles to some extent at the beginning and end of each year. The former often send up single blooms on a stem in spring and the hybrid teas send up clusters in the autumn. 'Royal William' is a very good example of the latter.

'Royal William's large, dark, semi-glossy leaves are rarely troubled by disease and make a very good background for the flowers. It was bred from a cross between 'Feuerzauber' (available in the USA as 'Fire Magic' but not on sale in the UK) and a seedling, so that we in Britain are left largely in the dark as to what has given its excellent qualities.

'Ingrid Bergman', the other rose that I mentioned as a possible top choice, was raised by the Danish hybridist Poulsen in 1986 from 'Precious Platinum' × a seedling, and gained a Trial Ground Certificate from the RNRS and a Gold Medal in Belfast and in Madrid, together with the Golden Rose award in The Hague, but it has taken it a long time to make any impact on the UK market. Gradually, however, word of mouth recommendation has made gardeners aware that it is probably the best deep red bedding rose of medium height, with only its lack of a worthwhile scent keeping it from the very top as an all-rounder.

SILVER JUBILEE

I well remember Alec Cocker, the Aberdeen nurseryman, at the conference of the World Federation of Rose Societies in Oxford in 1976 looking like the proverbial cat which has licked the cream. New roses were on display to delegates, varieties that had not yet been put on the market, and Alec had a bowl of a peachy-pink variety with blooms of immaculate shape. It was impressive to look at, but its creator, who knew better than anyone how it performed other than just as a cut flower, was quite certain that he was on to a winner. And how right he was. From the moment it was launched on the market in 1978 under the name 'Silver Jubilee', the Oxford rose has never looked back. The public quickly took it to its heart, not only because of its beautiful form and colour but because it grows so well almost anywhere in any soil and is very healthy to boot.

Expert opinion was the same as that of the general public, for it won a Gold Medal and The President's International Trophy in the RNRS trials, and a Gold Medal in Belfast and in Portland, Oregon. Later the rose was awarded the James Mason Memorial Medal.

I was a member of the judging committee at the time 'Silver Jubilee' went through the trials at St Albans and was one of those who marked it very highly, so I was rather mystified when later I tried it in my own garden, only to find that the flowers were smaller and fewer per plant than I remembered and that the growth was not nearly so vigorous. I put this down to the soil which, despite years spent in trying to improve it, is still pretty poor, but after I had

'Silver Jubilee' show off its shapely flower.

compared notes with other growers I was reassured. I was told it was a rather slow starter, and so it proved. It is worth a little patience.

The general good health of 'Silver Jubilee' probably derives from the German climber 'Parkdirektor Riggers' and the full parentage is given as ('Highlight' × 'Colour Wonder') × ('Parkdirektor Riggers' × 'Piccadilly') × 'Mischief'. The plant will grow to about 2½ft (75cm) upright and compact, covered with its fine, glossy foliage right to the ground. The immaculately shaped blooms are, as a

As a sturdy, healthy rose of medium height you cannot better 'Silver Jubilee'.

rule, of medium size, though there will be some that reach exhibition standard, so that 'Silver Jubilee' has done very well on the show bench. They last for ever in water, but a disadvantage when picking for a vase is that they often come on quite short stems and, even with those on longer stems, one has to contend with a phenomenal number of thorns. Again, however, it is worth it, and as a weatherproof bedding rose, with its exceptional freedom of flowering and continuity, 'Silver Jubilee' would be hard to beat.

As so often with a top-class rose, the story does not end there. Other breeders, as well as the firm of Cocker that originally raised it, have latched on to a good thing, and such varieties as 'Anneka', 'Armada', 'Beryl Bach', 'Castle of Mey', 'Cordon Bleu', 'Savoy Hotel' and 'Samaritan' have been among the first results of breeding with 'Silver Jubilee'. It may have been noticed that there is a mixture here of floribundas and hybrid teas. There are more in the pipeline in both groups.

SOUVENIR DE LA MALMAISON

The biggest and best bush of 'Souvenir de la Malmaison' that I ever saw was at Claydon in Suffolk. It was when my wife and I were touring the country for my book *The Rose Gardens of England* and Humphrey Brooke, whose garden we were visiting on this occasion, greeted us, at about eleven o'clock in the morning, with the offer of a glass of calvados. Ever eager for new experiences, we said yes and repaired to the summer house, at which point Mr Brooke discovered that he had locked himself out of the house and that his housekeeper was off in the village with the keys. So we never got our calvados, although we did get what we had come for, which was to see and make notes on a remarkable garden. Two things stand out; a truly phenonenal form of *R. moyesii* with no fewer than thirty-nine shoots coming from its base, which were very thorny for their first 6–8ft (1.8–2.4m) and then smooth, which will give you some idea of its size, and 'Souvenir de la Malmaison', which was one of the first roses to be seen as you went up the drive toward the house. Probably 8ft (2.4m) across instead of the more usual 4–5ft (1.2–1.5m), it bore (and bears elsewhere of course) with scarcely a pause all summer its very large, quartered, creamy-pink flowers, absolutely crammed with petals. Jules Gravereaux allotted it a special place in his Roseraie de l'Haÿ, where it was known as 'Queen of Beauty and Fragrance'.

One version of how it got its name is given by Nancy Steen, who recounts how it was sent as an unnamed seedling to Malmaison and much admired by a visiting Russian duke. He asked if he could take plants back with him to Russia and suggested that it

The beautiful blooms of 'Souvenir de la Malmaison' have ensured its survival since 1843.

should be called 'Souvenir de la Malmaison' in memory of his visit. On the other hand, it is also said that it was named by its raiser M. Beluze, who had some association with the famous garden. At any rate, it was introduced in 1843, a cross between 'Mme Desprez' and an unknown tea rose, from which it appears to get its fragrance.

The one drawback to 'Souvenir de la Malmaison', which can at times be very frustrating, is that the buds cannot always be relied on to open well in a

'Souvenir de la Malmaison' is a member of the bourbon family and so is recurrent.

climate with insufficient sun. The United Kingdom, on the whole, is probably too cold and too wet for it, but in a good summer it is pure enchantment. However, to help it along when the weather was not being too kind, Mr Brooke had the answer. He would squeeze each bud gently when it first began to show colour, and he told me of an old nursery hand he knew of who was paid sixpence per day for doing just that. He suggested that if I wrote about the rose I should mention this, and seemed quite surprised when I said that if I did prospective purchasers would head for the hills. In actual fact, in eight years out of ten – or thereabouts – there is no need to worry, and it will reward you handsomely for your patience during the other two. Surprisingly, in view of the above, the flowers produced in the cooler weather of the early autumn will be unsurpassed for quality and colour.

As a bush 'Souvenir de la Malmaison' does not, as explained above, reach more than 4ft (1.2m) in height, though spreading out quite widely. It benefits from the support of a tripod or other suitable frame, or can be grown against a low wall. Then there is a climbing form, which is rarely seen, but grows against the house at Charleston Manor in Sussex. This is considerably more vigorous than the shrub, but probably does not flower quite so freely. It was put on the market by the nurseryman Henry Bennett in 1893.

Nearly sixty years later, another sport, which had been growing and lovingly tended for a long time in St Anne's Garden near Dublin, was introduced by Hillings' Nursery under the name 'Souvenir de St Anne's'. This makes a bushy plant up to 7ft (2.1m) high with the most attractive semi-double flowers, white with blush tints; it is very free blooming.

SURREY

How does one define a ground cover plant? To me it should be something which, either through close planting or because it spreads naturally over the ground by rooting as it goes or by underground suckers, will form a dense carpet of leaves (preferably being evergreen) no more than 6–8in (15–20cm) above the ground, effectively covering any bare earth and so smothering weeds and preventing new ones from germinating. If it flowers as well, so much the better, but attractive leaves should be the most important feature.

'Surrey' is probably the best of the ground cover varieties named after counties.

If this is the right definition, there is no rose that really qualifies, although ever-increasing numbers are sold as ground cover plants. Some, such as the Gamebird series, which includes 'Pheasant', 'Grouse' and 'Partridge', probably come closest to my definition for they do spread across the ground, rooting where they touch it, and they do mound up after a while so that their leaves cover the surface pretty well. However, they do not keep them in place for twelve months of the year, which means that weeds can become established during the winter months of bare rose stems, and weeding among the thorns can be like putting one's hand into a tank of piranha fish. In addition, these particular roses are so vigorous that they are likely to outgrow their allotted space in a small garden very quickly. They are really best for what is known as amenity planting, in the central reservation between dual carriageway roads and in other similar places in need of decoration. 'Pink Bells', 'White Bells' and 'Red Bells' also have plenty of fine glossy leaves and flower well, though only at midsummer, but they can grow to 3–4ft (1–1.2m) tall, which is not, I think, what a ground cover rose is all about.

Most of the other ground cover roses, such as 'Red Blanket', 'Rosy Cushion', 'Candy Rose', 'Ferdy', 'Bonica' and so on are simply fairly small, bushy, wide-spreading shrubs which happen to cover quite a lot of ground, shading it with their branches but by no means excluding all weeds. However, if they are planted quite close together so that their branches to some extent overlap, they can give a pretty good cover. It is best, however, to think of

Economical to use, here only four plants of 'Surrey' occupy a sizeable bed.

them, not primarily in terms of suffocating weeds, but as attractive, low-growing shrubs which will make interesting and colourful garden features, perhaps grouped in threes or fours in the foreground of a general shrub planting or in a bed on their own. They can also be used for covering a difficult bank and, if they do prevent a certain number of weeds from making a nuisance of themselves as well, so much the better.

The best of the County series of roses come within this last category. They are a mixed bag, some, such as 'Surrey', 'Berkshire', 'Cambridgeshire', 'Kent' and 'Hertfordshire', very good, and some only so-so. Although grouped together as one series, they originate primarily with two different raisers, Kordes in Germany and Poulsen of Denmark, the latter being also the raiser of 'Pink', 'Red' and 'White Bells', and they vary a lot, differing a good deal in growth habit; 'Kent', for instance, makes a fine, rounded bush and cushion of white bloom in summer, but does not spread very far, and 'Suffolk' is much more upright than most of the others, almost a floribunda.

OPPOSITE: *'Surrey' comes into bloom early in the season and is seldom without flowers thereafter.*

Of them all, the best by a considerable margin is 'Surrey', which will grow to about 3ft (1m) tall and end up with a spread of rather more than this. It branches freely and is well covered with small, glossy leaves which so far have proved to be very healthy. The flowers appear all over the plant in both large and small clusters and are a soft pink, deeper at the heart and with attractively frilled petal edges. They come first early in the summer and the bush is then hardly without any until the autumn frosts. Prolific is the word that comes to mind when thinking of its performance: or profuse.

In referring to 'Surrey's health, I used the words 'so far'. This I did because these roses are still comparatively new and we are still learning about them. 'Surrey' is, in fact, one of the oldest, having been introduced in 1987, but most of them date from the 1990s. I have grown 'Surrey' now for three years and I am still experimenting to find the best method of pruning. I think on balance that a light, over-all trim is the answer, cutting back rather harder some of the stronger shoots that come low down on the bush and which, once their heavy cluster of flowers open, will actually brush the ground and the blooms may be spoiled by mud splashes after rain.

'Surrey' is the result of crossing 'The Fairy' with a seedling rose and is, I would say, a great improvement on it, good rose though 'The Fairy' is. To back up my own opinion on this I can add that 'Surrey' gained Gold Medals in Baden-Baden, Genoa and in the RNRS trials. It is reasonably fragrant and the flowers are weatherproof.

In case it should be thought that I am ending up on too much of a downbeat note, condemning the so-called ground cover roses for not being something they, themselves, never claimed to be in the first place, let me put the record straight. All the varieties I have mentioned are absolutely first-rate within their own terms of reference and make top-class garden plants, mixing happily with others, standing on their own or, in the case of the lower growers, being excellent for bedding. If used in this way, 'Surrey' will occupy the space it would take six or seven hybrid teas or floribundas to fill, so that it is extremely economical to use as well as providing colour for something like six months of the year. Who could ask for more?

INDEX